SONGWRITING ON DEMAND

- A methodology

Martin Carlberg

Original title: Songwriting On Demand

Editing by Patrick Rydman and John Woodall
Proofreading by Maria Ek
Layout by Maria Ek
Publisher: BoD · Books on Demand, Östermalmstorg 1,
114 42 Stockholm, Sverige, bod@bod.se
Print: Libri Plureos GmbH, Friedensallee 273,
22763 Hamburg, Tyskland
ISBN: 978-91-8080-954-2

"For a songwriter, you don't really go to songwriting school; you learn by listening to tunes. And you try to understand them and take them apart and see what they're made of, and wonder if you can make one, too."

— *Tom Waits*

THANK YOU!

Thank you all who has in some way assisted in the writing of this book. The most important names must surely be Patrick Rydman, John Woodall and of course my love Maria Ek without whose support I could never have done this. I also want to thank everybody involved in the production of the music accompanying the book. The five songs are found on the EP "Skywriting" on all streaming platforms.

The songs on "Skywriting" were recorded in Spinroad Studios by Pedro Ferreira.

Go Out On Your Own
Drums- Abbe Abrahamsson Piano- Stefan Wingefors
String arrangement and recording by
Mattias Bylund at Bylund Strings
Cello- David Bukovinszky
Violin- Hanna Helgegren and Mattias Johansson
All other instruments – Martin Carlberg

Can I Come Over & Crazy Town
Drums - Fredrik Oscarsson
Fender Rhodes - Joona Toivanen
Hammond B3 - Dan Helgesen
Backup Vocals - Maja Norming, Lisa Ljungberg, Per Strandberg
All other instruments – Martin Carlberg

Be Still My Beating Heart
Drums - Abbe Abrahamsson
Piano - Stefan Wingefors
Strings arranged by Mattias Bylund and Erik Arvinder
Performed by Stockholm Studio Orchestra
Conducted by Erik Arvinder, Engineered and
Recorded by William Bleeker in IMRSV Studios
Violin - Anna Roos Stefansson, Danial Shariati, Daniela Bofiglioli,
Henrik Naimark Meyers, Jannika Gustafsson, Jonna Simonsson, Lola Torrente,
Oscar Treitler, Paul Waltman, Simona Bonfiglioli, Veronika Novotna,
Viola - Christopher Öhman, Erik Holm, James Opie, Vidar Andersson Meilink,
Cello - Daniel Thorell, Filip Lundberg, Pelle Hansen
All other instruments – Martin Carlberg

Land On My Feet
Drums - Abbe Abrahamsson. Grand piano- Joona Toivanen
Hammond B3 - Dan Helgesen
Backup Vocals - Maja Norming, Lisa Ljungberg, Per Strandberg
Horns - Anders Carlsson
All other instruments – Martin Carlberg

TABLE OF CONTENTS

TABLE OF CONTENTS I
INTRODUCTION 9
A SUPER BRIEF BACKSTORY ON ME 21
PREPARATION 32
CREATIVITY 41
THE DISNEY MODEL 56
The Dreamer 57
The Realist 58
The Critic 59
THE ARTIST vs THE CRAFTSMAN 65
Art 66
Craftmanship 68
The Craftsman needs the Artist 72
SONG STRUCTURE 77
The Intro 79
The Verse 81
Rhyme schemes 83

The Chorus 86
The Bernstein Principle 90
The Last Chorus 97
The B Chorus 98
The Outro 99
The Ending 100
The Cookie 104
MODULATING KEY 131
STARTING A NEW SONG, SCENARIO NO 2 134
The Riff 134
LYRICS 146
STARTING A NEW SONG FROM LYRICS 153
CHORDS AND HARMONY 162
WRITING ON DEMAND 184
WHY RHYTHM IS KING 202
A SONG vs A "PERFORMANCE PIECE" 211
THE SENDER AND THE RECEIVER 217
HOW TO READ A BRIEF 221
WRITING FOR TV OR FILM 236
WRITING FOR A MUSIC LIBRARY 240
WRITING FOR A COMMERCIAL 245
THE FORCE OR STANDING IN YOUR OWN SHOES 246

INTRODUCTION

I think Master Classes are absolutely great. Just to hear and/or see a true master of a craft, any craft really, speak about his or her relationship to these skills and also about the insights he or she has spent an entire lifetime developing and gathering, is something I find truly inspiring.

But my observation is that these wonderful people, although being masters of their artform, need in no way necessarily at the same time be very good teachers of that said artform. Not at all.
It seems to me, that in spite of their musical mastery, they more often than not are pretty useless at actually explaining what it is that they really do, and how it is they really do it.
I especially remember an instructional video from the absolute genius, legendary guitar player/singer/songwriter George Benson, sitting with his guitar in his home, in front of his fireplace, playing a I-VI-II-V
(In the key of C Major that would be C-Am-Dm-G).

He then moves on to try and explain something about how to re-harmonize that chord progression in a chromatic fashion.

While trying to explain this concept, he gets *extremely* inspired by the music that is simply and effortlessly pouring out of him, much like water pours from a well. You could almost say that he gets high on himself :)

He finds himself quite unable to explain how that music just ..."happens".... in him, or even "to" him, since for him it is a thing of pure intuition. The creative state he enters is much like a hypnotic trance. He continues instead to go ever deeper into this creative state, and in real time and right before our eyes... All the while making highly exited exclamations like:

"Oooh, the possibilities are endless!!"

He goes on to play one re-harmonization of I-IV-II-V after the other, while still failing to provide a single shred of new information about exactly how this is done or just how any of it works. This is probably, because George Benson and other masters like him that perform on this for us mere mortals unreachable level, they are doing whatever it is that they do on an intuitive level, much more so, than on a technical one.

I believe that these exceptional people have long ago passed the level of "how" to do what they do. All the necessary knowledge and technical skills have already been long acquired and have been internalized so deeply that they are almost forgotten.

When reminded of a "how to" technique their eyes might turn unseeing for a moment, as they remember some ancient learning.

Then they might nod their heads, reminiscing in silence, that once, maybe they thought about it in such a mechanical way. Much like when Ben Kenobi for the first time in many years, hear the name "Obi-Wan", in the first (IV) Star Wars film. With exactly those same unseeing eyes he whispers in remembrance under his breath: "Yes, once I went by that name..." Therefore, in any and every traditional meaning of the idea of how to teach, George Benson and his likes (George Benson has no "likes", but you know what I mean) is, perhaps, useless.

But far more important, in another way, just to be able to observe these geniuses at play in real time like this is something absolutely priceless and holds a world of learnings. Learnings much deeper in a way than any traditional "proper" teaching of the sort of "first this, then that". It is the same as when in the 8-hour long The Beatles "Get Back" documentary, we find John Lennon late arriving at the studio, and Paul McCartney, while strumming and fiddling with his bass and singing nonsense lyrics, before our very eyes writes the basics of the title song for the documentary, the classic "Get Back".

Another perfect example for me, is watching another giant

at work, namely the great Hans Zimmer’s master class, on masterclass.com . It is actually a masterclass I would highly recommend. I truly loved it, along with Zimmer's highly philosophical approach. You should know this though about it: The 10 hours or so we get to spend with him in this piece, doesn´t have that much of "hands on" tips or techniques (there are a few, but just a mere handful.) It leans much heavier on Zimmer’s philosophy of film music composition.

This to me is the sign of a true master, that the person has, after accumulated enough knowledge and technique and whatnot, have moved on from the practicalities of "how" you do something, to the more esoteric "why" you do something. I absolutely love watching these masters at work. There is so infinitely much to learn from just watching them and listening to them.

As for myself, I must admit that I am not one of these masters. I am though, if I dare say so myself, in my best moments, pretty good. Perhaps even once upon a blue moon really good. Maybe, on a few specific things even almost great. (Easy now, tiger!)

This must be made perfectly clear: I am definitely no master, and I accept this as fact.

So, I don’t just love to consider the deep philosophical discussions and ponder on the issue of the "why". I also love the "how" and am in no way finished with it. I love to learn new things. I constantly actively seek learnings. Still we are all different, and when I recommended the Hans Zimmer Master Class to a Mixer/Producer friend that lives in and works out of Nashville, he then was so absolutely underwhelmed by it, since it did NOT have all the "how" bits, that he wrote an angry letter (email, of course) to masterclass.com demanding his money back. (Which he did!). This was because he did not care one bit for all these philosophical rants and ramblings. He wanted the nuts and bolts. He wanted stuff like: "if there is to be cello, at the same time as conversation, the cello needs to play in this range and not that range to make both music and words audible".

He wanted that kind of specific information, which is very valid stuff indeed, but more of something you might get from a regular teacher and not from a true master.

This is because the true masters are past that. Being merely an apt student myself, and as I now have stated clearly, not a true master, that might in a strange way make me just the right person to write a book like this. I might be the right person simply because I love both the "how" to do things and the "why" to do things, just about equally.
Be that as it may, I am in these few modest pages going to give it a go!

What then *is* music? I mean, what is it really? To attempt to explain that, is almost like trying to explain the universe. (According to the Japanese American string theory physicist, The Universe is music!) Sometimes you just have to humble yourself.

Sometimes you have to say: "I don't know."

Or... you say "To hell with modesty, let's try anyway!" Since that sounds like more fun, let's do that! And if nothing else just because it is such great fun to try to figure things out! We'll most probably fail in solving all or any of the great mysteries, but so what? If we assume there is an infinite number of "wrong" choices and explanations, and only one "right" choice, then the odds are clearly against us. Even so, let us make some assumptions that are against all the odds together! We will have fun along the way and will probably learn at least something, maybe even something of value!

> "Never tell me the odds! "
>
> — *Han Solo*

I have many stupendously talented musician friends who I feel, in many ways, are a lot more talented and skilled than I am. They might sing more freely with a more naturally pleasing voice. Quite often they may have much greater vocal range than I have.

They might play their instrument better and more expressively than I play mine or they might play multiple instruments with seemingly and disturbingly little effort (these people are probably the worst!).

They might have a better sense of time. (Musical time, that is... which refers to how you position you're playing in relationship to the beat).

They might understand the musical language of harmony better and improvise more easily and readily over intricate changes and odd meters in a way far beyond my capabilities, and so on.

I *am* quite sure, though, that I am the one among all of these musical friends of mine, who have had the highest number of songs published and released. Now, why is that?

Am I better at writing songs, or more talented at creating music?

No, I absolutely don't think that is the case, at all. Perhaps then, I am better at writing large *quantities* of songs? Or am I somehow more talented in *that* sense? A born "Quantity creator"?

No. I don't think that is the case either. So what might the answer be then? Not the answer to the question as to why I have written *more* songs, mind you. I don't think *that* question, nor its answer, is of any real interest to anyone. The real question I instead want to ask is this:

Why aren't these wonderfully talented people writing more songs?

Or, a lot of times, even this:
Why aren't these wonderfully talented people writing songs at all?

Well, maybe they just don't want to write songs.

If so, and for those that simply has no such desire, this book is not for them. This book is instead for anyone and everyone that do want to write songs. Or even for those who *want to want to* write songs. (Did you follow that?)

One clue to what the answers to these questions of why these wonderfully talented people aren't writing more songs or not writing songs at all, is probably found in the fact that I at times hear some of these friends speak with total dread and fear in their voices about the whole song writing process.

I have also often heard them being totally dismissive of themselves as songwriters, as they strongly will proclaim, that for some mysterious reason, they "have absolutely nothing to say". Well, I will stick my chin out and dare to say this:

I believe they are all mistaken. They are all wrong.
I believe they have lots to say.
I believe everyone does.
I believe you do, too.

Having the self-confidence that allows you to believe that you have something worthwhile to say, is merely depending on the quality of the relationship you have formed with the process being creative, along with how and when to be creative. Then comes also working on having the courage to show the products of your creativity to someone else. You need to be able to "let go of outcome" and dare to be, in a sense, "naked" in front of others.

Amazingly, a lot of the time, I think people succumb to the fear of showing stuff they have made even to themselves! That we cannot even bare to be naked in a room by ourselves! We are avoiding mirrors, if you will.

Showing your work, finished or in progress, to someone else, or as I said even to yourself, lays painstakingly bare some seriously uncomfortable truths about the present skill level of your writing and the quality of your ideas.

Or the perhaps most dreaded thing: the potential lack of actual quality in the ideas.

Add to that; when you haven't written songs that much or maybe not at all, writing a great, a good or even a passable song, might seem a task about the size of climbing Mount Everest. But writing a song doesn't have to be such a mountainous undertaking. It is my intention to help the reader of this book (you) by providing some of the ideas that have worked for me, in order to reduce that Mount Everest to nothing but a small hill that you can actually quite easily walk up and down, whenever you so desire.

In this book, I will be presenting my ideas and methods for songwriting in general, songwriting on demand, genre specific songwriting, and more...

One way to tie that to intention the title of the book, which is "Songwriting On Demand", is by this very notion, that the demand for the writing of a song can both be external, meaning some kind of "customer" or situation calling for a song to be written, or the demand can also come from you yourself.

These ideas that I will present, are not at all "truths" per se. Nor are my methods even necessarily "better" than any other method or set of methods that might be out there. My methods are not even necessarily better than having *no method,* if having no method is what works best for you. These words are simply the thoughts, ideas and methods that I use and that have given me somewhat consistently high and quick results. I present them to you with the humble hope that there might be something in there for you to take away, something that you can use and make your own. I also encourage you to and hope you can improve upon my ideas. Please do.

My views and methods are not set in stone, but are instead a constant work in progress, to be forever tweaked and fine-tuned. It is a labour of love, and it is never supposed to be finished.

When you have written something personal and artistic, the step of then showing that work to the rest of the world can for sure be highly intimidating. You are after all, by doing this, and in no small way, putting yourself on display to be judged by others. You are indeed in a way putting yourself in the line of fire. And for sure, often we can and will be quite harshly judged.

We all know it. We have all experienced it. People can be really mean. Because of this, raising your hand and willingly putting yourself up for that is some scary shit for anyone and everyone. Because infused in your piece of art will be *your* taste and *your* skills, (or indeed lack thereof). The work you put forward will reveal in full daylight your level as a craftsman, but also with no pardon, weather you perhaps fall short in any area of the process.

Note: To end words, gender specific with "man" like in "crafts-man" is archai and old, but I hope you forgive me for not re-inventing every such word in this book. I am perfectly aware that it might equally well be a "craftswoman"

> "I don't think about commercial concerns when I first come up with something. When I sit down at the piano, I try to come up with something that moves me."
>
> — *Lamont Dozier*

To be clear:

Your art will tell us deep secrets, both abstract and specific, about YOU. There is no way around that. But, it is the way it is supposed to be.

IT´S ALL GOOD!!!

I will also try to offer some ideas later on, regarding how to deal with such thoughts and fears. I sincerely do hope that the alternative way of looking at fear of criticism that I will offer perhaps a little bit of a different vantage point. And that it can prove as helpful to you as it's been helpful to me. As someone who now raises their hand, stands up, and by writing this book takes a step forward to address the world, it only feels appropriate to first ever so briefly, tell you at least something about who I am, what work I have done, and why it is so, that I *might* have at least some input to offer on the matter of "Songwriting On Demand".

A SUPER BRIEF BACKSTORY ON ME

I started to write songs pretty late, maybe in my late teens or early twenties (is that late? I realize that I can't really tell), and then got to release two albums. One album each with the two bands that I was in, Sweetwater and The Remedies, in the mid and late nineties. The genre for both these albums could perhaps be described as being somewhere in the neighbourhood of The Allman Brothers meets Steve Earle.

On these two albums there was no real co-writing going on. The modus operandi was more that each of us wrote their own stuff and then brought it to a rehearsal, showing the tune to the band, learn to play it and then immediately press the red button and record it. I remember that I wrote only a few of the songs on the Sweetwater album and maybe half of the songs on The Remedies album. I would definitely say that the songwriting for these two albums, was my first real taste of writing anything at all.

Almost immediately, as I recall, something in me was hooked. I was hooked on this feeling of magically conjuring something from nothing

I just tried stuff to see what happened by listening… inwardly… outwardly…and seeing what transpired… just by emptying myself... and opening myself up to the "endless possibilities", (as George Benson might put it), then -voilà! Out of thin air, where there was nothing, something suddenly… exists!

I then and there fell in love with the feeling of where I might come up with an idea, perhaps a riff or a melody, or it might be a rhythm or a special chord change. The magical feeling being, that it didn't even exist a minute ago. This rush changed the course of my life completely.

And then, to work on that idea, that magical something, to polish it until it shines… or to tinker with it until the mechanics of it works, is a passion that has never lost its appeal to me. It is a rush, a natural high, a wave on which to surf.

> "...brought on by a Simple Twist Of Fate. "
>
> — *Bob Dylan*

But at the same time writing songs is often a work of agony. It can hurt. It can be so incredibly difficult. I guess though, that that's an important part and aspect of it all. If it was easy, and if it was always easy, the result wouldn't have the same worth, would it? And, just to balance this romantic picture, sometimes you realize later than you would have hoped, that the piece of magic that you are polishing is actually a turd, and it will remain a turd no matter how shiny you make it

So, after that first initial experience, I wrote, and I wrote, and I wrote. I came up with truckloads of crappy songs. I used to always carry around this recording Sony Walkman and sing fragmented ideas into it whenever they came to me. This though, is a really really GOOD practice! The only thing that differs nowadays is that the Walkman has been replaced by a smart phone. I have, in recent years, gone through these old cassette tapes, in search of a possible forgotten or overlooked gem, but alas, no. It was indeed as I feared mostly crap, but that's all good and fine.

However, from all these hundreds of songs and ideas for songs, at least a few decent ones crystallized. Maybe even half a dozen to a dozen good ones.

Those songs were recorded and released on two solo albums: "Crashlanding" in 2006 and "Bonne Chance" in 2009. They were both released by a major label (Universal).

Then after that I went on to record another album on that same major label in 2012, but with a trio called Bag Of Tricks.

The album was simply self-titled after the band. For everything that was written before Bag Of Tricks, there had definitely been no method of any kind to my writing process. All touch and go. Just working on songs until they were solid enough sketches to attempt rehearsing and recording them with a band. But to keep things in perspective: There is definitely also something to be said about that loose way of working. And because of that...

This feels important to make clear again:

There is no better or worse way to write songs.

You don't really necessarily need a method for writing songs.

There is no better or worse way to write songs.

At least not until you DO, and there IS.

There are a million and one ways to do this and they're all good. All methods have merit, and it is important to keep in mind, that all of these various ways will all lead to slightly or vastly different outcomes. Meaning, whatever approach you take to the process, will absolutely and always affect the outcome. This book is essentially about different ways to make the process of writing songs easier and more time efficient. These methods of mine were, as so often is the case, born out of necessity, when I found myself in the situation of having to write a lot of music steadily on a day-to-day basis, and often with really short deadlines. These methods have made the work easier for ME. Bottom line, that´s really all this is.

But what does it mean to make the writing process easier and more efficient? Well for one, it doesn't necessarily mean that the songs that come out of that process will be better or worse, but they will most definitely be *other* songs, different songs than the ones written with more hardship. It might lead to different takes and different results from the same "idea material".

**Making it easy on yourself will yield one result.
Making it hard on yourself will yield another result.**

So, take from that reasoning what you will. All, nothing or something. But anyway, back to the story...

> "As far songwriting, my inspiration comes from love, life and death, and from viewing other people's situations."
>
> — *Ed Sheeran*

One might say that writing the songs for the Bag Of Tricks album, flicked some kind of a switch in me. It turned on the lights, if you will. The Japanese call this a "satori moment". Which apparently if I am rightly informed, roughly translates as an "Aha!" moment, a moment of enlightenment.
It all happened roughly like this...

We, the band, Bag Of Tricks, did a simple rehearsal, just the three of us. Bass player Bertil Holmqvist, drummer Fredrik Oscarsson and me, just trying riffs and grooves. I always have at least two hundred or so unused riffs and

musical ideas, melodies and stuff, just like I used to have on my Sony Walkman cassette tapes, only now they're on my iPhone voice memo. A good time was had by all and we all got into an easy flowing creative mood.
I recorded that rehearsal on that same iPhone and brought it back home to pick these recordings apart to see if anything of value had actually happened, what it was we had actually gotten "on tape", and if any of it was stuff worthy of the work it takes harnessing ideas into a finished song.

Fast forward to ten days later, when I called Bertil and Fredrik to say that we could start recording, since I had finished writing an album's worth of tracks from those rehearsal fragments. They were surprised, to say the least, but the real point here is, so was I.

In the studio we then went almost immediately, and in a few days of recording time that eponymous album "Bag Of Tricks" was done, dusted, and in the bag (pun intended).

Note: "Eponymous" is a fancy word for "self-titled". I didn't previously know the word, but my editor John, wanted it there).

The 'aha moment' that I had gotten from this explosive outburst of creativity and fast paced songwriting, was something like: "I can really do this... And it is almost *easy* if I do it in this certain way". So what was that certain way that I had found worked for me? That is exactly what I will try to get to the bottom of in these pages. And as I said before, maybe just maybe, there will be something in there for you to take away.

> "My style of songwriting is influenced by cinema. I am a frustrated filmmaker. A fan once said to me, "Girl, you put pictures in my head!" and I took that as a great compliment. That's exactly my intention."
>
> *— Joni Mitchell*

To me, the feeling of "flow" is a natural high and a lovely state to be in. How that state is accomplished, both randomly by itself when it magically wants to appear, and on purpose, is a thing we will definitely have reason to come back to later on.

Perhaps an ancient quote from a Roman philosopher can be used here:

> "Luck is what happens when preparation meets opportunity..."
>
> *— Seneca*

"Preparation" in this case would be both life experience, personal disposition in general, but also more specifically, having all these saved up riffs and musical ideas on my trusted Sony Walkman to work with. I also keep this little nice leather notebook full of lyrical ideas, one-liners, sayings, as well as little poems and such. I used to carry it with me everywhere I went, but lately, I've got into the habit of writing stuff down on the iPhone notepad instead. Every now and then I will go through the notes on the phone, taking note of the ideas that still strike me as good or that at least makes some kind of sense, and then after that, I transfer that material to the notebook. Lyrical ideas that is.

The "opportunity" here that "preparation" met, was of course teaming up and jamming with such great and inspiring players as Fredrik Oscarsson and Bertil Holmgren!

The writing of this album was my first taste of the songwriting method that I would start to develop from that moment. I will continue to develop and refine this for as long as I live and breathe, since it is, of course, not something that could ever be "finished".

I have used this method to write perhaps 1000 tunes, of which maybe 800 or so have been published. About 500 of them can be found on Spotify and other streaming sites. My songs have appeared on countless Swedish TV-shows, series, commercials and so on. I am not that incredibly successful on Spotify, but my catalogue combined generated about 20 million streams in 2023, and that number increases every year.

As you can see, I am not the "one-hit-wonder" guy with that one career defining big hit song. I off course wish that

I had had a really big hit song, but at least instead I have written a lot of them. I have written great many songs that "work", songs that do what I intended them to do and that leads us to the main thing this book is going to be about:

Craftsmanship.

The artistic quality and uniqueness of the ideas themselves aside, this is not what these pages will focus on. Instead, I will write about ways to in which you can handle ideas, any ideas, how you can with craft and skill, form these ideas into well-shaped songs. If the ideas in your heart, or your head, by chance also happen to be ideas of great quality, all the better!

I also sometimes get to teach these ideas in music universities in Sweden. That teaching situation is what led to the idea of putting my ideas down on paper in the form of a book.

The music I have written is in a great many different genres and styles: Pop, Rock, Hard Rock, Blues, Jazz, Singer-Songwriter, Folk, Latin, Reggae, World, and so on.

This leads me to the conclusion, that this methodology of songwriting works in every style and genre. That is probably because it simply has nothing to do with style. Instead, it has everything to do with communication. It is based on general principles of how we as people communicate. Whatever the form of communication, there are commonalities and traits, ways in which we receive and process information. These general principles of communication serve as my guidelines. That and gut feeling. If I had to make due with one though, I would go with the gut.

Sum of all sums: Gut feeling is and will always be Numero Ono, and this or any other book, is complementary. Having said that, and without further ado, let's dive right in!

Or, maybe just a little further ado, that last passage gave a feeling in my gut that I need to take that thought a bit further and make this following small disclaimer:

There is no wrong or right in art. There cannot be. It is a direct contradiction of terms. There are magical components to great art in general, that no given method can ever guarantee. Even if you use this method, or any other, to write a perfectly structured song, that perfect structure need not make that song a great song. It will probably make it a good song. Or at least an okay song. Greatness is and has always been an elusive and mysterious thing. However, if you are a person with genius ideas, some parts of this book might help you find the right structure when crafting those ideas into great songs. Because it is quite possible to write a crap song even on a brilliant idea. Skills matter.

The quality-of-ideas in art cannot really be taught at all. Only the craftsmanship side of it can be taught, and this too has its limitations as we do not in any way know all there is to know about that which we try to teach.

I think I will repeat once more that with other words:

No teacher knows everything there is to know about what he or she teaches.

So, write and create to your hearts content, in any way, shape or form you want to. Make every "mistake" in the book, there might be some "happy accidents" in there. There will certainly always be learnings to be had!

A book like this has only one use, and that is for the writer to share what he or she thinks about the world and what strategies have worked for *them*, so that you may benefit and hopefully get some new vantage points and fresh ideas. I will tell you what has worked and what has not worked for me. Use it if you will. Discard it if you will. Please improve upon it. It shouldn't be that hard to do! (There can be other uses for a book like this, I later realized, like using it as paper weight or similar!)

Whenever I read a book of this kind, or when I watch a Master Class, or study in any other way, I see it like this: if there is but ONE take away in the material, one really good idea to take with me, then that is GOLD. That little piece of gold makes it all worth it, both the money as well as the effort. I am always in search of those golden nuggets, and I sincerely hope you will find one or two of them in this book. If not, either I have failed miserably to convey these golden ideas properly, or you might just be a fucking idiot.

We'll have to wait and see.

PREPARATION

In a general sense, everything that happens in life, is what constantly and every day prepares you for making art and is what gives you the "stuff" to make art from. This always simply IS. Life cannot *not* do that. But to be more specific: proactive preparation to write songs is, in my mind, a matter of always being on the watch for things happening around you, big or small, things that could be used in the context of a song, and to create ways to save those little ideas, observations, riffs and snippets in practical ways for later use.

Always have your "radar" on! Pay attention!
And for sure, to pay attention in such a way is surely an acquired skill, that needs to be practiced and developed over time.

For both musical and lyrical ideas, I try to always be on full alert, ready to up interesting rhythms or melodies or chords or choices of words. For instance, when Samuel L Jackson in the 1998 movie "The Negotiator" says: "*Crazy is on the bus!*"

Crazy is on the bus???

That line went straight into my little leather notebook!

I think I might have mentioned it earlier, that little notebook of mine. I found a really nice pretty one with a little leather string tie around it. I opted for a fancy and classy beautiful and posh notebook for a reason.

That nice little leather book makes me feel that I am in some way "honouring" my connection with my "Muse", whatever that may actually be... and that it in some way shows my respect and reverence for the creative process. This might sound strange, since I other times within the pages of this book, will say things that might indicate just the opposite of respect and reverence. I might say that it's all merely a nonsense game of making up random things, just for the fun of it. I genuinely think both vantage points are equally true and need to be in put in some kind of balance in the mind and in the soul at all times. Or maybe not all the time, I realize when thinking about it. Maybe sometimes it's actually preferable to lean one way or the other.

> "All is fair in love and songwriting."
>
> — *Norah Jones*

That is in fact a point that needs to be made. That sometimes you absolutely need to be rebellious, bold and daring. Sometimes you need to respect nothing. And other times you need to ask nicely, or the muse will refuse to come out and play.

Sometimes what you are creating might feel like it is the most important piece of true art that has ever been manifested in the history of the Universe, and you would without hesitation die a thousand horrific deaths before you would let anyone change a thing about it. At other times the creative process needs to be allowed to be carried out more in "committee".

I know other writers who feel that such a fancy pants leather notebook is the absolutely wrong way to go. That for them, it makes the writing process more scary, turning the idea of songwriting, already a towering mountain to climb, into an even higher mountain, making also the threshold higher before they can bring themselves to face that dreaded blank empty page.

So, each to his or her own. But I most strongly recommend you find a solution for stocking up and saving up on ideas that suits you and works for you.

> "I respect any and everyone who dares face the blank page and not look away."
>
> — *Anonymous*

Sorry, I just made that quote up. It is true though. And there are a lot of these quotes about the scariness of the "Blank Canvas", dating back hundreds of years.

As for me, these days I use a combo for saving the lyrical

ideas that I might stumble across, or that just pops up in my head. Like I said previously, I no longer carry with me that notebook at all times. I instead write stuff down on my iPhone memo and then maybe once a month will I go through my phone notes and transfer whatever scattered lines feel as if they are worth keeping to the notebook. The rest I promptly delete.

This means that the things in the notebook are ideas and lines that have been vetted and curated and have survived not one but two levels of elimination. That means the stuff in there is bound to contain lines of good quality. 99% of everything in there will have *some value to it.*

I will talk more about how I use the notebook in later chapters, but I stress, that for me a notebook it is absolutely invaluable to have.

Even though maybe only about 10% of the times that I go looking for stuff in it, will I find something that I then use verbatim, it is still like I have said invaluable, because at least 80% of the times, lines in it will trigger and feed my imagination, firing new trains of association, which will in their turn so very often lead me to the lyrical idea I need. And that ain't too bad, is it? Here is another tip for finding lyrical ideas (probably the best "tip" ever): Read. Read a LOT. Read novels, read quote books, sayings and books of idiom. Take classic sayings and turn them on their head. Read poems. Read lyrics of album sleeves to songs you don't know. Take titles of songs, books or anything and twist and distort them.

All of those examples and a thousand more, are ways of looking for ideas outside of yourself. Looking for ideas outside of yourself, is something you can occupy yourself with in creative low-tide periods. In the "in-between" periods of creation. If you find yourself in a period where ideas are pouring steadily from an internal well, none of that outside searching is probably needed.

But even still, there is something to be said for keeping the input volume of ideas up. Even though this stuff is collected from outside yourself, there is something personal in the selection process, and the bigger you make the collection of these little one-liners and such, the more that collection is going to reveal something quite true and personal about you. On the music/riff/melody side of ideas, I use the iPhone voice memo thing. Currently I have maybe something in the neighbourhood of 250 ideas in there. I definitely should take the time to record whatever is good out of that into an "Musical ideas" Pro Tools session.

I actually do this sometimes, but it is time consuming and boring, so I have not done it in a while. It would surely suck if all those ideas were to be lost… so I will do it tomorrow. Perhaps. Hot DAMN it would suck if I lost some of the stuff that's on there. So maybe I will. Yes. Maybe tomorrow…

On the music side, ideas do not have to be played on an instrument to be recorded. For me it's important to catch them in the moment. So I sing riffs, vocalize grooves as well as melodies and lyrical ideas to catch that lightning in a bottle. (Or sometimes when the idea is not that great: catch that fart in a jar!)

For exercising and starting up the musical ideas, to me it's often very beneficial to expose myself to music and really all kinds of art forms that I don't really understand. Maybe I won't even try to understand. Because... you absolutely don't always have to understand art. Just expose yourself to all kinds of artful expression and see what you experience. How does it make you feel? What does it stir in you? Whatever the answer may be, it is all good when you want to fire up your creativity.

> "Stir It Up, little darling, Stir It Up, oh yeah"
>
> — *Bob Marley*

The purpose of such exercises, apart from it being an overall good thing to expand your relationship to art, is it's importance for immediate songwriting reasons. You will be loading and filling up your sub-conscious to the brim with all these unsorted impressions.

This built-up dam is holding a flood of currency for creativity. It will sit there as potential, like a savings account. Just like you need to put funds in a bank account if you wish to be able to make a withdrawal at a later time.

And when you have that subconscious, all bundled up with

impressions, all you need to create magic, is a quiet space and time.

"Space", meaning, where do you write? It is nice if you have a designated room, a little den or a beautifully lit studio where you can go and write in perfect undisturbed solitude and stillness, but that is something most people don't have. Most people's lives don't look like that. Yours might or might not. So then you have to face this cold, hard truth:

To write is a decision.
Let`s say that again, and in big fat letters:

To write is a decision.

If you want to write songs on demand, it is not possible to idly wait around for the times you can ride the lightning of inspiration, that just once in a blue moon and seemingly by chance arbitrarily shows up. No. You absolutely must not wait for inspiration to come to YOU. You must go to IT. As Hamlet might have said: "To write or not to write, that is the question". So if your answer is "YES" and you decide to write, you will need to be able to write wherever you have to write and whenever you can write. It might be on the bus to and from work. It might be on the train or in a café. This is easier when writing lyrics than music, of course. We are all aware that it is not really kosher to sing out loud or have a musical instrument with you and sit and work on musical ideas in public places, but if you are able to work on musical ideas all in your head, or in written notation, that is an awesome skill.

If you are anything like me though, you have to make sounds out loud. So if you need to make sound which will be regarded as unwanted noise of other people, you need to find a secluded place. Any secluded place. Paul McCartney and John Lennon wrote early Beatles songs in the bathroom of McCartneys childhood home. That is solid proof right there that any room is fine. If there are multiple choices available, then try difference places to see if it makes a difference. You will probably find that some places will have better vibes for writing than others. If you can, find a place with really good energies. Good "Feng shui", if you will.

But I most definitely still think it is best to be quite flexible about it and not be too picky about the location, in order to preferably be able to write anywhere and anytime, if you "have to". So seek out the places that make your muse seem the closest to you, but don't be enslaved and limited by the idea of such a place. Stay flexible.

Try going outside, if the temperature and weather permits where you live.

The same goes for "time", meaning you will write when you can. Whenever you can with no excuses. That being said, it is a rare talent, or a skill to be practiced, and acquired, to just be able to switch hats from your "everyday hat" to your "song writing hat" and turn on and off the faucet of creativity at a moments' notice just because an opportunity to write presents itself. If you can learn and hone this skill, awesome.

Good for you!

Very few can, though, so for the rest of us, it is a good idea to plan our writing sessions. Set aside time when you know you will be undisturbed, and can allow the creative, more right-brained part of your subconscious to come forward, to get you in that owing state of mind which makes the magic happen.

So let's look some more into this fantastic phenomena that we call...

CREATIVITY

I remember one warm day, it might have been the summer of 2010, I was wandering around kind of aimlessly (or more accurately, I do not remember my errand or reason for being there that day, it is not that I have a habit of wandering around without purpose) in the streets of my hometown Gothenburg, when the thought and the feeling came to me, that I was completely out of touch with my muse and therefore with the whole process of songwriting. I had no musical or lyrical ideas coming to me. Had I perhaps lost the ability to write? Would I ever be able to write again? I could not feel "it" in me. I thought that it was… gone.

Which of course, it wasn't.

This was well before I had formulated any kind of method. I had, in that moment, nothing to hold on to. It's not that you necessarily need a method. Sir Paul McCartney himself says, "I don't know how it's done"…

Now I know better than to get scared when I feel like this. If I've been away from writing for a while, it feels as if the faucet of creativity has been turned off.

Now I rest assured that the faucet will just as easily come

back on. Just because you don't go fishing in the pond, that doesn't mean that there are no fish in it.

This alone makes for a good reason to have a method for your writing and to avoid being a slave to the whims of your muse throwing you crumbs of inspiration if and when "she" feels like it.

> "Each song has its own secret that is different from another song, and each has its own life. Sometimes it has to be teased out, whereas other times it might come fast."
>
> — *Mark Knopfler*

A method always gives you a place to start. It shows you a way in. It gives you an access point.

I have often heard these questions asked: Where does creativity really come from? From within? From without? Is it divine? Are we divine? Or is it just our subconscious minds talking to us? And if so, who is really talking to whom?

Phew!

We can only speculate as to where from creativity origins. We can only believe. But instead of getting bogged down and caught up in that rabbit-hole of a discussion, even though it is an incredibly interesting one, let's focus on how this creativity thing seems to work. Let's try to examine and learn from what it actually DOES rather than question what it IS. Several great creators have said that it's simply a matter of "getting out of our own way", and I do think there is a whole lot of truth to that statement.

> "We need to get out of our own way."
>
> — *Unknown and unsung genius*

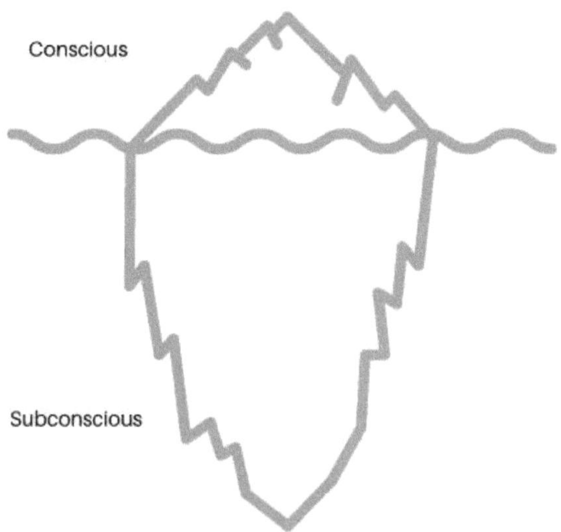

Or to put it in another way. the conscious mind needs to get out of the subconscious mind's way. And when it does, voila! Flow state!

The conscious mind is slow. The subconscious mind is at least 10.000 times faster. John Cleese, who is a creative genius in his own right, has given great lectures and talks on this matter, some of which can be found on YouTube. I greatly recommend them as they are a great watch. He has also written a book on creativity called "Creativity; A Short And Cheerful Guide".

One thing he said really stood out and has stayed with me. I think it went something like:

"You must make a quiet place for yourself where you will be undisturbed."

Actually that wasn't the quote I was looking for, but he said that too and it is also true, so...

The one I was thinking about goes something like – and I apologize if this is not verbatim –

"You must have a willingness to stay with the discomfort."

This means, at least in my interpretation, that the creative work will get uncomfortable at times, and you need to be okay with that. It will be hard, painstaking work sometimes. It will even be physically painful at times. Jimmy Webb even went as far as saying:

"Songwriting is Hell on Earth. If it isn't, you are not doing it right."

I do not really fully agree with that somewhat sombre and binary view of the matter. Songwriting doesn't always have to be Hell on Earth. Sometimes it's even quite easy and enjoyable. Those moments should of course be savoured, though. They can be few and far between! I feel the need to back up a few steps and nuance that last bit some more. For me, writing is actually for the most part enjoyable, but it can, and will be, a painful struggle at times.

So it's important to make peace with that and to get comfortable with being uncomfortable. The point is just that. It CAN be hell on earth, and you shouldn't be afraid of that. You absolutely need to learn how to stay with that tension. Expect it. Work through it. There will always be fruit on the other side of it. There will as the saying goes, always be sun behind the clouds. Maybe the fruit, or the win, the gain, on the other side of that struggle (the discomfort, as John Cleese put it), might just the knowledge that a not-so-good song has been written, but you have to write those too. You have to. They are part of the discomfort. You have to have the willingness to work through that wall of resistance. Do that en masse, and you will without a doubt write better songs. This "You must have a willingness to stay with the discomfort" motto, I would like to propose, is also applicable to life in general, in our relationships, arguments, and so on.

We could even go as far as to say that no growth or development of any kind is possible without some level of discomfort.

No pain, no gain.

John Cleese is a genius.

Let's therefore all get comfortable with at times being uncomfortable.

Maybe at times, when we have struggled our way through the discomfort, the song that we find on the other side is, despite our perseverance and efforts, no good. There are simply no guarantees. But then again… there's always the next time.. Maybe then the song on the other side of that rainbow is one of your better ones. Maybe it's your best one yet. Maybe it's a freakin' masterpiece…

Back to this quote then:

"You must make a quite place for yourself where you will be undisturbed"

This is the first, and probably the most basic, fundamental thing. You must create a time and space where you can write and be undisturbed. With that said though, what does "undisturbed" really mean? If you have the capacity to completely go inside your own head, this can work perfectly well as long as the people in the room leave you alone.

Paul McCartney (have I referenced him before?) is said to have written many of his numerous masterful songs in the room with other people just hanging around.
If you are able to work like that, congratulations.

(Also, if you can write songs like Macca, congratulations).

Still, the optimal circumstance for most people, I would have to assume, is a quiet solitary place, and ample time to stay there. Optimal circumstance that is, for allowing the creative process to kick in, for the faucet to be turned on. However, what happens when that creative flow state happens? What makes flow happen? Can it be called upon on demand?

Here is a little more personal background on that matter before we get back on track with that important question:
I have been a long time study of different views of the concept of the subconscious mind. And during the pandemic, since I had little or no music work, I decided to finally complete my studies to become a Hypnotherapist.

I then went ahead and opened up a private practice in Gothenburg doing exactly that. Hypnotherapy. This in much simplified terms means that I perform therapeutic work on people while they are in what could be called a hypnotic trance. This also means that I have had a lot of training and now also practice in the relationship between the conscious mind and the subconscious, or unconscious mind. The model that now follows is quite over-simplified, I am well aware of that, but I believe it is still accurate enough to be relevant and close enough to the truth to serve as an illustrative model of what is going on in our heads.

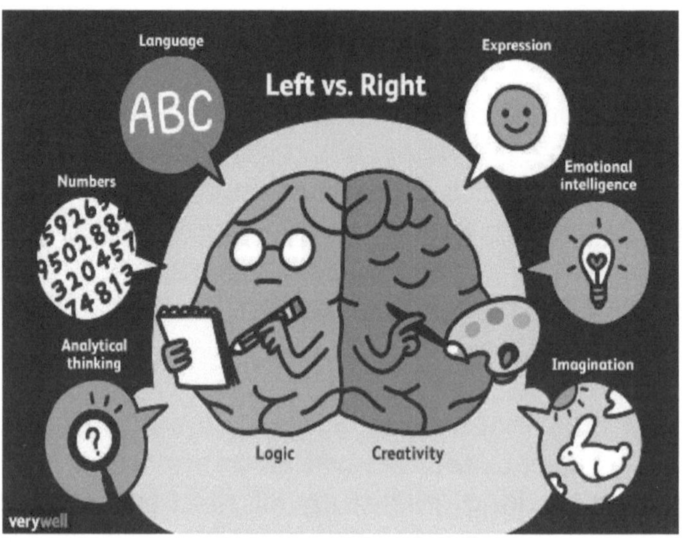

The left part of our brain is the home to our more logical functions, like language, analysis, critical and orderly, specific, linear thinking. The right part of the brain is more emotional, visual, intuitive, abstract and, you guessed it... creative! Both brain hemispheres have need of each other to make one complete and functional human being. One way that the right creative mind needs the critical left side, and that is of particular interest here, is for the function of protection. The right side of the brain has little to no consequence thinking.

That makes it extremely open to the power of suggestion. Gullible, even. Therefore, the left side filters incoming information, and inspects it, before allowing it passage to the right hemisphere. This function is crucial to not "fall for anything".

This is your internal voice of "wait a minute, this can't be right!", or that creeping feeling of doubt and scepticism. However, this system is not a function with a perfect track record.

It fails quite often and leaves us feeling foolish or feeling that we have been tricked in some way. Our left-brain critical filter also protects us from saying and doing the wrong thing at the wrong time. This is, of course, to stop us from making complete fools of ourselves. Once upon a long time ago, this could even have meant the difference between life and death. It could have meant the difference between being included or being excluded from our tribe or group. It can probably mean life or death even today, in many places and circumstances around the world, when I come to think of it. This verbal filter is also most surely less than perfect. Perhaps you can recall times in your life when you have said just the worst possible thing or chosen the perfectly wrong response in a given situation. I think: "Yes".

In order to really get those creative juices flowing and get into the much desired "zone" or "flow", this critical filter or critical faculty, if you will, must be turned down or preferably switched off completely. How is this done?

Well, it might take some practice, for starters. We are all differently conditioned to access this state. The left brain needs to know that it is safe for it to let the right brain come forward. In order for it to know that it is safe, it has to *learn* that it is safe. One example of how the left side of the brain can learn to deem it safe to open up for the right side of the brain, is clearly seen when you are watching a movie. Your left brain knows that what is being presented to you is fake.

The right brain doesn't. The left brain knows that just above the upper edge of the picture, there is microphone on a boom stand and a person managing it.

It knows there are multiple cameras, lighting, and a director with a screenplay in hand telling the actors to do one more take. Everything is shot in fragmented scenes, edited together and then music is added to enhance emotion. But as long as the telling of the story is good, the left brain shuts up about all of this. It pulls away.

Steps back into the shadows in silence to let our creative right brain enjoy the story as it is being told. Unshielded and unrestricted by the critical left brain, the right side will feel sad, exited, amused, scared or whatever emotion the filmmaker has set out to make us to experience. Imagine the same state of being receptive to incoming information in the same way as when you are watching a great movie, but for outgoing information. Then you are receptive and non-critical towards information coming from the inside, from your heart, your soul and your subconscious.

Let me repeat that: The same way that you can put aside criticizing stuff coming from the TV, you can put away criticizing stuff coming from within. Your own ideas. And if you can put away or temporarily suspend your internal critic when needed, you can then enter a state where you can immediately act on impulse, without any second guessing, without ever asking yourself, "is this a good idea?" or "what will others think?". In this state you will have the shortest distance possible between the creative mind and the executive mind. This creates a situation where there are no hiccups between "thinking" and "doing".

I was on this songwriting retreat once upon a time, early in my writing career. This was before I really got into writing songs all day and every day for a living. I think I had perhaps just recently released my first solo album "Crashlanding", and that that album was what made them ask me to come. On this retreat the participants where put together in groups of three. Each member of this trio having a designated role. These roles were the obvious: "Producer", "Music" and "Lyrics".

For this three day retreat, having a new constellation each day, I was always cast as the "Lyrics"-guy. On day two (if I remember it correctly), the "Music"-person was a very successful Nashville songwriter. I will not drop his name, but the year before he had won a Grammy for best song of the year. In other words, he was pretty big time. This was a real education. I kind of stood in awe as he just... did his thing...

He was a really basic strumming guitar player. Just barely enough of a guitar player to even be called a guitar player. Yet he just banged away on his really nice blonde Gibson Hummingbird, trying on each and every idea for size, in real time, ideas owing one after the other at a high and steady pace. He was no natural singer. Yet he sung as if there was no tomorrow and this was his last day among the living.

The ideas that flew by were nothing special, yet there was a feeling of searching and digging for gold. Or maybe one of those missiles that hone in on their target. I think by now you get the picture and where I am going with this story.

If it is not as clear as I think, the moral of the story is this: He just flat out DID IT.

He didn't (at that moment) have a single self-conscious bone in his body. And in this fashion he wrote about 300-400 songs a year. A lot of them where most probably pretty mediocre. I can tell you that the three co-writes I got with him were, well... bleak. But of course, some ideas, when you pound them out like this, are bound to be good. Some will even be great. Many will be recorded. A very few might become hits. As I said, one of his songs even got a Grammy (or it might actually have been as many as four Grammys). You will have heard this song many times. So is this the only way of doing it? Is the only goal to become a song writing machine that goes for the win though the sheer number of songs written?

No, definitely not, but I think it is a good, or even great, example of one way this can work. So you see, I definitely think this "getting out of your own way" thing is absolutely crucial. Key. Paramount. Of greatest importance.

Muy importante. Am I making myself clear?

If you are someone whose creative juices are constantly flowing and who can just sit down and go at it at any given time, good for you! For the rest, here follows a short routine that can be used when those juices need some extra help to get going.

Exercise 1: Mindfulness.
Wherever you might find yourself, take a minute or two to really closely and mindfully observe your environment. Try to really take in every detail, the aesthetics, colours and so on. It doesn't matter if you are in a familiar or brand new place, this mindfulness exercise will make your mind ready to also notice and pick up on feelings and signals coming from within yourself.

Exercise 2: Automatic writing.
Just start to write the first thing that enters your mind. For some this comes easy, for others it takes practice.

There is to be no censorship or filter. No weighing your words or judgement. Just write absolutely anything for a few minutes.

If this exercise is hard for you, ask yourself why that is so.

If it is, your self-criticism has got an unhealthy hold on you that you need to break.

If so, more of this and not less is prescribed.

The purpose of the exercise is to liberate yourself from self-doubt and put your inner critic on hold for the duration of the session.

Exercise 3: Doodle, draw or sketch.
About the same explanation as for the previous exercise, only this time it is about drawing randomly or at least the first thing that enters your mind in order to spark your imagination.

> "I wish I were one of those people who wrote songs quickly. But I'm not. So it takes me a great deal of time to find out what the song is."
>
> — *Leonard Cohen*

Exercise 4: Singing random lyrics.
This is for those who, like me, have a notebook for lyric ideas.

If you do, open it and start to make choruses out of random lines. Try one and if it works, keep going! If it doesn't, swap the line for a new one. Try to make the music fit the lyric.

Or, I take that back. It is not only for those with a lyric notebook. You can of course free base improvised lyrics of the top of your head.

The notebook is to use previous work as a spark plug for igniting your creative engine.

Exercise 5: Singing along with previously record musical ideas.

Kind of like the previous exercise, only this time you go through the snippets of recorded ideas on your phone (or on any other recording device), to see if anything inspires the continuation of that idea. If so, go for it! Ride that wave for all it's worth. If not, it might trigger something else.

Exercise 6: Make up a beat with a drum program of your choice and riff to it.

Exercise 7: Just riff for a while.

Exercise 8: Try to find what your current mood sounds like. Give your current state a soundtrack.

Take a second or two to turn your attention inwards and just sense what your current state feels like. Then try to find a chord that matches that state. Or a groove. Or a melody. Or a riff. You get the idea. Be particular. Is this chord closely enough resembling my state? Or does it need some extra colour to get it right? Is there more than one chord needed to match the state?

Another way of looking at the whole creative process, that might help you find your own handle on it, is the following interesting model.

THE DISNEY MODEL

This is for sure a very interesting model for creativity, based on assuming these different perspectives:

#The Dreamer (visionary, idea supplier)
 # The Realist (maker)
 # The Critic (quality manager)

The model is just one of many similar models (another being for instance Edward de Bono's "Six Thinking Hats" to name just one), that all seek to describe the different positions or vantage points one can take in a given situation. Each position has its own merits at different stages of a given process.

A slight but important difference between these two is that Edward de Bono's idea was that he suggested six thinking styles (or "hats" to wear), which could be used interchangeably to suit one's needs, whereas The Disney Model follows the same sequence every time.

(This being said, do go ahead and feel fantastically free to do exactly as you please!)

The Disney Model was first developed as late as 1994 by the Neuro Linguistic Programming (NLP) great, Robert

Dilts. One of the basic, early ideas of NLP, was that much is to be learned from studying the strategies of successful people, and that by modelling their strategies we can find similar success ourselves.

So, Walt Disney's process (as described by Robert Dilts) goes something like this:

First you start out, by taking on the role of The Dreamer . This means there can be no second guessing yourself. No self-criticism at all is allowed at this stage. It is pure brainstorming time. Anything and everything goes!

> "If I want to say anything, I write a song. I think people who create and write, it actually does flow – just flows from in their head, into their hand, and they write it down. It's simple."
>
> — *Paul McCartney*

The Dreamer

In the "Brill Building" in New York, the home for many top songwriters dominating the U.S. charts in the early 60s, the legend says that on the wall in every writing room there was a sign saying:

"In this room there can be no mistakes"

To me this translates as:
"In this room you are The Dreamer and not The Realist or The Critic"

The enormous advantage of this is that you get the creative juices owing much more easily and go into a state where the ideas keep coming in a steady stream. So just get it out. Remember, NO JUDGING! No judgment at all. Every idea is a good idea. Get words on paper (or on your laptop or wherever). Get melodies and chords and arrangement ideas out there. Ride that wave or waves for as long as possible. Some days they only last a little while, some days they last all day long. Some days there is no surf at all, but for me, finding waves to ride has become easier with practice. The Flow state, as you see, can be interrupted from the inside as well as from the outside. And this is what criticism is at this stage, an unwanted interruption to your flow. Don't do it. Don't go there. Keep the water running. Be playful. After you feel done with this phase. When you have exhausted it, then and only then it is time to go to the second phase.

The Realist

This Realist phase, the way I see it, is mainly about the arrangement, the instrumentation and the production. It is about considering the receiving end. It is about the reality of the presentation. It is about giving it its best chances for being well received. How will it be performed and by whom? What instruments will be used? How it will be recorded, and so on. It is about how I can present this song, taken into account who it is I am aiming to present it to? And if I feel that the song needs a big arrangement and production, which might be costly in terms of personnel and studio time, do I have the funds to follow through on that? And even if I do, is this the song to motivate spending that much?

Because of this, for me, this phase that Walt Disney placed as the second phase, instead comes last.
Edward de Bono in his "Six Thinking Hats" to present the idea of these different thinking positions to work from, and saw them as interchangeable in order, while Disney had a fixed sequence. If we are to choose one way it is for me always the way with more personal freedom of choice. So 1-0 in de Bono vs. Disney!

(Sometimes it can be a good thing to impose limited choice upon yourself in a situation, but this is also, if you think about it an expression of free choice)

The third phase in Disney's model then is:

The Critic

For Walt, if I am not mistaken, being The Critic, in this way related to The Realist, meant to a great extent taking the point of view of the end consumer, and in his case, that meant the audience. This, of course, taking the point of view of the audience, is just a mere guessing game for anyone, although some have more of a knack for it than others, and if one pays attention to trial and error, one can definitely improve this skill. But even the best at this has a low success rate...

The main difference between The Critic and The Realist might be that while The Realist is more concerned with how to best present the finished product, in our case the song, (and therefor in my way of thinking is best placed last), The Critic is instead concerned with the quality of the ideas themselves and the quality of the structure and individual parts of the song.

For me, it has more often than not meant going over the material at hand, with a critical eye and ear, to see what The Dreamer really came up with this time. Quality checking it.

There are a thousand and one questions that can be formulated, and which questions that are relevant to ask, depends on who the " customer" is. If the customer is me, and I am simply writing a song for my own pleasure, I need only concern myself with my own taste.

I should then only aim to please myself. If I am writing for an audience that is used to my music being in a certain genre or style, I might cater to their expectations, to appease them, or I might go in the opposite direction, and try to surprise and challenge them.

If the customer is instead a publisher, I need to make sure

the song has the correct elements of the genre of the brief received by said publisher. Is the language, the groove, the melody, the chord choices, the arrangement and so on in style and context of that genre? The same thing applies if the customer is a company in need of a song for a commercial or any situation similar to this, these questions are always relevant:

#Does every component of the song do what it is supposed to do?
#Does the song convey the intended emotions?
#Does it do the job and carry the propel the song forward?
#Does the song as a whole feel complete and satisfying?
#Does the song and its parts have a natural flow?

For me, again the order of wearing these "hats" is almost always: Dreamer, Critic, Realist. This is because I think you can in most cases separate the song itself from its production, and The Realist only needs to come in at that later stage.

Another vital and crucial tool is in a way the opposite of everything said so far, about the importance of not being disturbed, which is to take breaks.

Do take breaks.

They can be short breaks. Maybe just a coffee, or perhaps or a lunch break. Gotta eat, right?

It could be as simple as deciding to put down the pen for

the night and come back to continue in the morning. A break could or should, in a way, count as a sort of disturbance or interference, right? Actually, and interestingly, no. When you take breaks when you really need to, or perhaps even before you really need to, the creative mind will keep working in the background, and might present the solution you were looking for, when you return from the break to work on the song Sometimes, even a even better solution might arrive, one you didn't even know that you were looking for. Interesting, right?

It's like trying to remember, say, that actor's name in that film, what was it called? You just can't remember so you leave the question unresolved, feeling like it is an itch you just aren't allowed to scratch. Then the next day, while waiting at a red light, out of the blue, it just pops into your head: *Jean Reno in The Big Blue!*

Sometimes this process is called a Trans derivational Search, and is, as you can probably see, an invaluable tool in any creative process. One method that takes advantage of this hidden processing power is to review your work just before going to bed, in order to revitalize what the open ends, untied knots and questions marks of it may be, by giving your unconscious mind the best possible chance of knowing what to do, while you sleep. There are countless stories told about this phenomenon. Remember, for instance, that Paul McCartney woke up with "Yesterday" complete in his head one morning. And that the lyrical idea for "Let It Be" also came to him in a dream. (Damn that guy's name keeps coming up!!)

> "Coming up, Coming up, yeah
> Coming up like a flower, Coming up, I say."
>
> — *Paul McCartney*

Mick Jagger (another one of these old geezers!) can be shown doing just this, when he gives us a glimpse into his writing process in the documentary about the recording of his solo album "Goddess In The Doorway". At the end of every day, he will sit down and sift through all of his unfinished song ideas. He tries them out, seeing how they feel and what else might be in them by just blurting out whatever comes to him in the moment.

It sounds easy enough a thing to do, but to a lot of people it isn't. I am one of those people.

I really have to get in the right mood to be able to do that. But I strongly believe it is a fantastic quality and skill to have. Practice this. Learn this. It will strengthen your connection to your subconscious mind. Oil the hinges to its door. It is as if we are still being judged by someone even though we are alone in a room. Learn to be comfortable with yourself as the audience. Learn to make that audience less judgmental in the creative "Dreamer" phase. Or learn to not to mind what it thinks.

So, let us try and sum up this short chapter on Creativity:

#Make an effort to create a private, tranquil place for yourself, where you can write.

#If such a place is not available right now, write wherever you are anyway. Don't postpone. Don't make excuses.

#Don't criticize or second guess early on when writing a song. Let the ideas flow unfiltered, unhindered and uninterrupted.

 # Take breaks. This allows you to come back "fresh", even if it is only after a walk or a cup of coffee. Often, for me anyway, if I take a break and take a cup of coffee or go for a walk or a run or go to the gym, I'm still in a creative trance. This, for me, means that ideas keep coming while on the walk or running or at the gym. I keep my phone with me, finding myself standing in these places singing musical lines, riff or lyrics into my phone. I might look ridiculous, of course, but what else can I do?

Ok, so let us move to something completely different!

THE ARTIST vs THE CRAFTSMAN

"Writer's block is a simple case of caring too much or too little about your work."

—Jimmy Webb

I think I might have said it earlier, that we all need to find our own place in as good enough balance between the two opposites of "it's all just a little game of making shit up" and "the art I am making has got to be the most important thing in the history of the universe".

Life itself is full of these dualities, balancing one thing off against another. It might very well be the most fundamental structure of this relative universe. Everything needs its polar opposite. By this relationship the parts that live in between (in practical truth, all matters, situations and things) are defined.

So as the headline says, herein lies a duality most relevant to our topic of songwriting, that I find interesting. The duality of Art vs Craftsmanship.

To see why it in my mind is so, that these two are in

absolute polarity to each other. we first need to decide on a definition of each of them. Definitions needs to be made as clear as possible.

Art

So, what *is* art really? It is an elusive concept. As such, sometimes one needs to start by looking at what something is *not*. One definition of art I have invented for myself goes something like:

> "Art is anything made with artistic intent and that has no other intentional function."
>
> — *Martin Carlberg*

(Ain't it something when you sign your name under your own quotes?! Pure narcissism!)

Well, whoever thought this meme up didn't really spend enough time on it! (Coughs!) There can probably be exceptions made to this. Art can absolutely possibly maybe be created by accident and without apparent intent, methinks. *Wouldn't such a thing in that case constitute a sort of immaculate conception of art?*

Another nuance:

> "Bad art reveals everything."
>
> — *Martin Carlberg*

(Again!!??)

That means art should ask questions rather than give all the answers. Leave something for the observer's imagination. Intrigue the beholder. Give them an "IN" to the art. Present them with an open door. Make them, the beholder, a co-creator of the piece in their own mind and from their own experience. That process will mean that the beholder or recipient will always, and I mean ALWAYS, misinterpret and misunderstand your work, and them doing so is a part of the grand scheme!

This is also true in life in general, innit? Questions are way way way way way way more interesting than answers. As soon as you get the answer to a question, you go: EUREKA! YES!! Only to go immediately looking for another question to keep your mind working.

What then, *is* bad art? And why is it bad? Is there really such a thing as inherently bad art? It is not an easy thing to define, but perhaps I would say "a thought not fully followed through". Not taken to its limit, or at least taken pretty far, is....bad.. (Could that have possibly been any more vague.

Maybe art that has a low emotional and/or informational input and is badly conveyed, is just plain bad.

(This reasoning doesn't really hold water, I can hear that myself. This IS a tough nut to crack.)

Who am I, though, or who is anyone really, to judge? Maybe I am just not "getting it" when I call something "bad art". Maybe the same goes for you? So perhaps we can, just for the sake of this little thought-experiment, simplify and sum it up like this:

"Art can be absolutely anything. But in its absolute and most pure form can have no other intentional purpose than the artistic expression itself."
-Martin Carlberg

(This MUST stop!!)

Craftmanship

So now as we look for the polar opposites of the Art vs Craftsmanship, and having now covered the art part, we come to the element of craftsmanship. Craftsmanship (in this particular definition and for this purpose), is in its essence i say, about function.
The point I am driving here is that function opposes art. Let me say that again. Function is the opposite of art.

For example: A craftsman receives an order to make a thingy. That thingy needs to have a particular function, and the craftsman needs to construct and make a thingy that fulfils that purpose. Or maybe the craftsman might get another order to make another thingy from a received design or plan. It is then not up to the craftsman to add, change or take away anything from the design or plan he or she is given, but the job is to deliver it as commissioned with the most meticulous attention to detail. The craftsman might, if called for, and if it is appropriate given the relationship with the particular client or customer, offer comments on the construction or the design, in the event that he or she notices any flaws and/or shortcomings with it. Or if he or she see ways to improve upon it, but in essence, the great and true craftsman will deliver exactly what is commissioned and asked for. No more, no less.

What this means and why this matter is of course because all of us must always in every given situation find our balance between these two opposites.

Or even better put perhaps, we must all find our favoured position between these two extremes.

Even so, most of us will find ourselves most of the time, sliding along that ruler. Very often balancing over in the direction of the craftsman. This will likely be for commercial reasons. If you aim to be a writer on demand, you will have to get comfortable leaning over strongly to the craftsman side.
Some people call this "selling out". I say that need not be

the case. It *might* be that you are "selling out", but not necessarily so. Whether or no you are "selling out", I think depends on your feelings towards the given situation. If the current or general situation makes you feel violated and dirty, as if though you have prostituted yourself, then yes, perhaps you have sold out. At least it will mean that for YOU it means you are selling out, and this type of feelings should be avoided in life for both your general mental health, as well as for the health of your "muse" and the health of your relationship to your muse. On the other hand, if taking on a more craftsman like approach seems interesting and inspiring to you, and if you find such a situation a learning and giving experience, then you are not selling out in any way. Not in any way, shape or form. Don't succumb to some kind of politically correct agenda, putting yourself on a high horse of alleged morality, dictating what is ok and what is not.

I have found myself to be highly flexible between the position of art and craftsmanship. Is this the same as being morally and ethically flexible? Perhaps it is. I can of course only speak for myself, but in my case, I don't think so. Why I can flex this way with maintained "muse-health", I suspect is mainly because I tend to differ between "my own art" as in "music that is to be performed by me as an artist", and "commissioned work", which is music that is to be "sold" and has an agenda and therefor has a craftsman purpose and quality.

The Artist NEEDS The Craftsman because:
In the absolute majority of cases, if you are like I suspect

most people are, you will probably want your art to be communicative. You will want it to be approachable and accessible to others, at least to some varying degree.
A spectrum of the "senders" (or let's use the word "Artist") intentions might look something like this:

#I want the observer/receiver/listener to understand exactly what I mean.
#I want the observer/receiver/listener to understand some of what I mean.
#I want the observer/receiver/listener to have a feeling of abstract understanding. Even if he or she don't get the exact particulars.
#I just don't care how it is received. I just wanna do my thing.
#I don't need to bother with being communicative. My art is the best thing since the discovery of fire or the invention of the wheel.

If you are Artist 1-3 or somewhere in that region, you will absolutely definitely need a good set of Craftsmanship skills to make your art communicative.

If you are artist 4, it's all good. Do your thing. Whatever makes you happy. You need to accept, though that if anyone is ever to receive what you are sending, it is purely by chance. BUT. Strong medicine can be made this way. Strong art. Great songs.

If you are under the illusion that you might be 5, I daresay, you are not.

(WHAAAT!!?? THE NERVE!! HOW DARE YOU??!!)

Well... I dare say so simply because Artist 5 (the Dylans, Lennons, McCartneys and such), would never find themselves reading this book. They would just do what they do. Books be damned. But, since you are in fact reading this book: You are unfortunately probably not among the likes of above-named gods, but instead you are human. You want to communicate. You want to write songs that make people feel something. And it can always be repeated one more time: there is no right or wrong way of doing this. There are, however, always possible lessons to be made regarding what have worked and what have not worked for others that went before us.

This is all this book or any book like it is or could ever be.

What learnings about what we do now can be had from those who did it before? Let us, since we can, stand on the shoulders of giants! These pages are just me writing down what has worked for me. Some ideas are my own original ones (only a mere few), other ideas are learnings I've picked up that have worked for others, and that I am simply passing along. Paying it forward.

The door swings both ways, and:

The Craftsman needs the Artist

If there is a design or a blueprint handed to you by a "customer" to follow, then "The Artist" in you that wants everything done his or her way, probably needs to be momentarily suppressed. Put on hold. Suspended. Tucked away. Sometimes there is to be absolutely no changing or tinkering with the design. But if you are to come up with an idea from scratch, which is often, or even almost always the case, then the question one might ask is:

"Where do ideas even come from?"

Well, I would say that they come from "The Artist" in you. "The Artist" can in this case almost be directly translated as "the creative part of your mind".

So, we now see clearly that the pragmatic Craftsman needs the magic of The Artist. Nobody but The Artist can magically reach out and grab a fistful of thin air only to then open it again, revealing, where seconds ago there was nothing, a beautiful pearl. Or a... stone. Or at least, a piece of clay or... well, something to work with.

A place to start...

The idea of The Artist vs The Craftsman (or The Artist *AND* The Craftsman, must we be so confrontational?), also gives us a way to deal with, and relate in a healthy way, to criticism.

Every one of us will receive critique. No one is spared. Some people simply loves to criticize. They can't help it. The itch to have an opinion is soooo strong. Also, when we criticize, it is understood in an implicit way, that the one dishing out the critique can understand and oversee the full meaning and scope of your work and in their elevated brilliance, know better.

And how these people simply seem to LOVE to “know better”. I honestly feel that this following vantage point, or way of thinking, has been extremely helpful in making me, I dare say, almost bulletproof to critique.

And I mean that in a good way.

I by no means mean to say that I do not listen to criticism. I do. I listen and listen good. I might even say, "interesting, please tell me more". And if I find something of constructive value in there, I absolutely keep it. But the difference is, through my little technique, I am able to not take any of it personally. It doesn’t “get to me”. It doesn’t push my buttons. It doesn’t make me feel bad. At all.
This might sound easy, obvious and self-explanatory, but why then, if it is so easy, do I still see so many of my esteemed colleagues suffer greatly when they are being criticized.

Therefor learning to handle being criticized strikes me as important.

The way I relate to this subject is as follows:
Firstly,art itself art cannot really be made subject for criticism. As art can be anything, like I mentioned earlier, and if somebody doesn’t “get it”, and gives your song critique, whatever they have to say still says nothing about

the quality of the "art part" of your song. It can mean only one of these things:

#They just don't like music of this type or genre.
#They don't like the lyrics.
#They don't like something in the performance or production.
#They just weren't in the right mood for your song.
#They just don't like YOU.

Conclusion: Not everyone can like your music. This will forever be a given.

So if someone attacks your music from an artistic stand point or just declares that it is plainly and utterly "bad", this only means that they fit one or all of the categories above. It gives you quite a lot of information about *them* but says nothing about your music.

And if they criticize the artfulness of it, it only means that they have a poor understanding of what art is, and that art in and of itself is irreproachable.

BOOM!!
This viewpoint just made you bulletproof to critique towards your art!

If, on the other hand, somebody criticizes the craftsmanship of your song, or the production of it, or the performances on it, this can instead be valuable feedback. It could once again be just a matter of preference and taste, and probably most often is, and then you can just let it pass, just as we did with the "art critique". But if you are lucky you can sometimes get useful knowledge from feedback.

The Craftsman in you should always want improve and seek ways to improve. You should never ever adapt the belief that you know enough. Therefore, don't be sensitive about this type of criticism. Instead, why not try being curious. Ask for more details. Like I said earlier, say "tell me more". Soon enough you will know if their opinion is a thing of value or just somebody who doesn't understand that their opinion is just that: an *opinion* and not in any way objective truth.

And if people are rude and mean in their critical judgement of you and your work, know this: They are only telling you about themselves. They are only telling you about their need to put others down, and this time you happened to be the one they take out their inner feeling of smallness on. This is truth. If you take away nothing else, keep this.

BOOM!!
That just made you bulletproof to critique towards your craftsmanship.

Combine these two ideas, and you have made yourself immune to all the negative energy that could live in both the sender and the receiver of criticism. Whether or not someone is actually trying to put you down or just trying to be straightforward about your work!

SONG STRUCTURE

I think that it is a really good thing to have a well-developed understanding of how songs usually and commonly have been constructed through history. At least the recent history of the last 100 years or so. Because if you do, you can then choose to use or discard or expand upon these song construction models as you see fit. In my own experience, it is much better to have an expansive bag of tricks, and only on occasion and once in a blue moon have to open it to take out a tool or a trick to use, than it is to not have that bag of tricks at all. It seems to me as good practice, often or almost always, and as soon as possible in the writing process, to get a grasp and an idea of what structure the song you are trying to write should have.

So, I thought I would go through some of the basic song structures of the last 100 years or so, and their inherent dramaturgic pros and cons. But first, let's look at the lingo (language) used when talking about song structure:

Most commonly we use capital letters, with **A** often meaning the first main part of a song. In a vocal tune this most often refers to the verse.

Then we have **B** meaning the second main part of a song, and in vocal tunes this is most commonly called the chorus

C then, will refer to any additional third part of a song, whatever that may be, like a vocal Middle eight or an improvised solo or a written instrumental part.

And so on, of course, in the cases there are even more parts to a song. Therefor song structure schemes can have basic looks like this:

AABA

ABABB

ABABCBB

What is not used normally, but that I would like to add here in my book is the use of these two acronyms:

Firstly:

i, which will be used for "intro".

I will use a lowercase letter i instead of a capital letter I, because the capital letter I can easily be mistaken for the roman numerical I meaning the "one" which is often used for describing the root chord of a harmonic (most often major) key.

Secondly:

P meaning Pre-chorus

Often a verse will not transition smoothly into the chorus, and need the help of a short section designed to perform this task.

So why it this good knowledge? It is really a study and understanding of at least some sort of communication and the way people in general like to have things presented to them.

Starting off a song, we have a few different possible choices:

The Intro

We can have a separate intro part that is not repeated anywhere else in the rest of the song. Most often when this is used, the part is instrumental, but sometimes in certain genres, for instance the Cabaret genre, there is sometimes a half recited half sung (often rubato), vocal intro. Like a prelude or a presentation of sorts.

Example of Instrumental intro with spoken word: Let´s Go Crazy -Prince

Example of Instrumental intro with strings: At Last – Etta James

Example of Instrumental intro with riff that is only used as intro: Panama - Van Halen.

The intro could be a riff that serves as a big hook in the song.
Example: Smoke On The Water – Deep Purple

Or the intro could be using a part of the chorus.
Example: You Give Love A Bad Name – Bon Jovi

Or, we could use the verse chords and just wait 8 bars for the vocals (or melody instrument if it is an instrumental tune).
Example: Everybody Wants To Rule The World – Tears For Fears

Or we can use dreamy sounds to create an atmosphere that serves as an entrance to the mood we want the listener to be in when we then begin to tell our story.
Example: Brother In Arms – Dire Straits

Or we can skip the intro altogether and dive straight into the telling of the story.

Example: Hey Jude, Long Tall Sally

Ok... Moving on to the Verse :)

The Verse

The Verse is generally viewed as the "storytelling" part of a song. So, the first verse then, needs to introduce us to the story, setting and plot as well as to our main character or characters of the song. The first verse needs to let us in on the premise of the song. The situation our hero, anti-hero or villain is in. His or her mood. His or her view of the world. Options or lack thereof. And so on. (Or, the first verse can just throw us straight into a story with no introducing or honey-mooning! Songs are also allowed to be void of all sense-making!). The most usual way to write lyrics, is to write in some kind of rhyming meter (Duh).

It is not absolutely 100% necessary to rhyme, but since it is arguably the strongest and most easily accessible way to lend language elegance, weight, impact and power, I would say that *that* is the reason 99.999% of all songs ever written, have been written in rhyme.
But while rhyme is the most obvious way to give your lyrics both sway, style and heft, it can also be a direct line to the land of cliché and smelly cheese. How to discern? Gut feeling, I guess. Which really doesn't help much. All one can do is keep at it. Again, gut feeling. If rhymes you are coming up with make you cringe though, then it's... not good.

This humble book will not even try to be an all-encompassing or an even particularly comprehensive coverage of rhyming patterns. There are plenty of other much better sources for that, but what I will do, is to include some basic groundwork. (Also, this basic groundwork is most probably all you will ever need in this matter...)

Having said that, let us "dive in" and swim briefly in these waters.....

There are actually more than one way to rhyme. Firstly there are different types of rhymes; some sources will list more types than I will here, but I find these four to be the ones of main importance:

#The Perfect rhyme. This type of rhyme is the strongest and has both the same ending vowels and consonants. Like in STRONG and WRONG or POWER and TOWER.

#The Additive and Subtractive rhyme. This type has the same vowel sound but added or subtracted are consonants. Like in AIR and STAIS.
#The Family rhyme is perhaps not as strong a rhyme but opens up to field a lot. It uses vowels thar aren't the same but sound similar or the same. Like BAIT and LATE.

#The Assonance rhyme is more of a near rhyme... CAT and BAG. Use with caution and rarely.

Rhyme schemes

A rhyme scheme is simply a pattern of how the end words of the lyrical lines rhyme with each other. Rhyme schemes provide a construct for your lyrics to fit in. If you stick to a chosen pattern, the listener will automatically, on a subconscious level, recognize this and start to feel comfortable and "safe", this is because or brains love when it can place "trust" in the repeating pattern it has detected. To know at least a few different rhyme schemes is a very valuable part of any songwriting tool kit. The easiest and most fundamental rhyme scheme is probably this:

A

A

B

B

This means that the last words of the first- and second-line rhyme with each other, and then the last words of the third and fourth and so on.
Like this:

A businessman asked me if I could make up a rhyme
I said "Of course I can, but it'll cost you dime"
He told med "No problem, I'll pay by the phrase"
I said "I'll get right on it, if that is the case"

I realize that there is a clear possibility for confusion here, since I am using the capital letters A, B, C and so on, both for defining parts of a song, as well as the individual lines in a rhyme scheme. But since this vocabulary is the one commonly used, and you might find it elsewhere in both literature and in practice, you might as well get used to it here too.

The next pattern up would be this:

A

B

A

B

A businessman asked if I could make up a rhyme
I answered that I surely could
He muttered "It will probably cost me a dime"
I said "Ain't that just as it should"

A third pattern is this next one that is seemingly the most basic of all. But is still used less frequently than the first two. It goes like this:

A

A

A

A

Example:
A man asked if I was a maker of rhyme
I told him "I am, but it will cost you a dime"
He said, "money is no issue, what matters is time"
And if you fail to deliver, I will view it a crime"

The Pre-chorus (sometimes called a Bridge)

Sometimes when the Verse is done, the song itself or the lyrics or the melody simply does not feel "ready" to move on into the Chorus just yet. Something in the build up is missing. At these times four, or even eight bars, of a separate and new part might be needed to make a smooth transition from verse to chorus. The reasons to insert a pre-chorus can be either musical, say for instance that the verse is not able to build enough and the transition into chorus is too abrupt.

Or the last chord of the verse is the same chord that begins the chorus and there is no change. The musical reasons to insert a transitional part like this are many. And since the job description of the part is to work as a bridge between the verse and the chorus, why not simply call this part "The Bridge" and be done with it?

More often the name "Pre-chorus" is used though, so I will use that. Or, as I said, the reason to infuse a pre-chorus can also be lyrical. Perhaps there is still some missing information in the story, so it's not quite ready to move into the chorus. The chorus often being a "summing up" of the intention of the song. Let's say there is not enough story told yet at the end of verse 1. Then a pre-chorus might be a good way of solving that.

The pre-chorus works as and is written as a problem solver, and adds precisely what is needed to transition to:

The Chorus

> "Don't Bore Us, Get To The Chorus!"
>
> — *Per Gessle, Roxette*

So now we get to the Big Dog. The part of a song, any song, that people arguably most often will remember (or forget to remember if it isn't good enough!). This is the part that more than any other part, makes or breaks a song. The chorus is most often the "essence" of the song. It often holds the story of the song boiled down to a conclusion of sorts. It can be a single word repeated. It can be a few words or a sentence. It can have a rhyme scheme. But the most common trait of a chorus is probably that it "lifts" the energy of the song. That it "takes off" and gives a "release". That it is catchy. Hooky. Memorable. The "sum" of the song.

The "concept" of the song. The amalgamation.

This description is very likely at least a common way to view the chorus. If you want to go in another direction with your chorus, you can, and I firmly believe you have the universe's blessing and permission to do so.

A trick that often works, is to have the lyrics doing the opposite in metrics of what the verse does. For instance, if the verse is "wordy", i.e. is packed with a lot of words, try to write the chorus to have few and perhaps sustained words. Or vice versa.

If the verse is just comprised of a few long sustained words, it might be a good idea to make the chorus more word-dense. If both the Verse and the Chorus have the same "word density index", it might be a good idea to go the opposite way in the Pre-chorus.

Example of word-dense verse and not so word-dense pre-chorus: Genie In A Bottle -Christina Aguilera

Here is a little, but in my mind, quite significant songwriting "hack". In fact, to me this is a gem:

When starting to write a new song from scratch, try starting by witing the chorus first.

I favour this over starting with writing a verse for these following reasons:

Using this method you don't move forward until you have a strong chorus idea. And this you will be needing anyway, right? Consider the opposite method – starting with the verse:

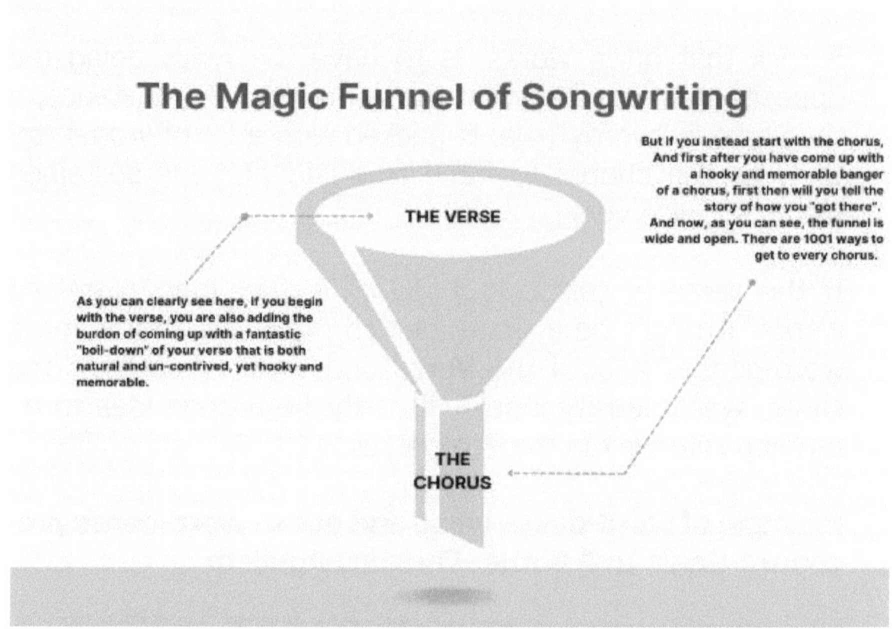

In this case you begin telling a story in the verse that you then will have to find a really strong and clever distillate of in the chorus. Everything you have said and played so far in the song must now be summed up, boiled down and polished to a shining diamond. By this, you are in a way painting yourself into a corner and creating a situation for yourself with fewer options available. Fewer options than what? Fewer options than if you view the chorus as the "destination" of the song. Since, if you start at the destination, there are most likely multiple ways of reaching it.

So you make the chorus "this is where I am" and then you let the verses be the story of how you got there. A picture I like is that of a funnel. Writing the chorus first puts me in the narrow end going to the open end.

Caveat:
You might not even WANT to write a "chorus" song though. And if that is the case, then never mind this part. Or you might even sometimes WANT to make it harder instead of easier on yourself and work diligently on finding that really poignant distillation of your verse. There can surely be a point to that as well.

Now we have gone once around the basic form of the song. The first verse and the first chorus. When I have been to songwriting retreats, this following occurrence is something that has happened more than once: In the afternoons or early evenings when all the little designated groups of the day gather to show and sing and play for the others what songs had been made from thin air that day... Every time they had played once through the form intro to first verse and first chorus of their newly written song, there would be a spontaneous round of applause. Especially so, if the form was an elegant one.

And at this point I think a communication "rule" comes into

play. As always, feel free to break this and every other rule… still, I think this next one is a great one to know. I heard this one coined by the great Leonard Bernstein, who made a series of educational videos featuring a full symphony orchestra playing various musical examples of music principles with him teaching and conducting the orchestra.

Amazing. This must have cost a fortune and would of course be an impossibly sized production for teaching music today.

This principle (let's call it the Bernstein Principle) goes like this:

The Bernstein Principle

1. **Introduce**
2. **Establish**
3. **Alter**

What does that mean?

If we continually Introduce new parts in a song, there is no larger structure to latch onto. If you are writing avant-garde, that might be exactly what you want, but if you want people "onboard" in another way, the Bernstein Principle is awesome. It is valid at any level of zoom, from zooming in on melody phrases, as in:

You play a few notes (**Introduce**)

You play them again (**Establish**)

You change it up a bit (**Alter**)

Or, the principle works equally well when zooming out and viewing song structure. In this case, we have by now introduced the structure of Verse-Chorus, and according to the Bernstein Principle, we should established that pattern by doing Verse-Chorus again. Does this correspond with reality? Well... Only 99.999999 of all Pop or Rock songs work this way, so... yes. The intro is sometimes just a set up and "doesn't count" Or it is often used in full or in an abbreviated version as a brief interlude. This gives our song this structure thus far:

Intro

Verse

Chorus

(Perhaps abbreviated intro as interlude)

Verse

Chorus

Or

i A B (i) A B

Since we now have both **Introduced** and **Established**, it might now be a good time to **Alter**.

If we go into another round of Verse-Chorus, we risk ″over establishing″ and lose the interest of the listener.

This leads us to a delicate moment in song arranging. When we have **Introduced**, **Established**, and now need to **Alter**.

There are quite a few options here:
The Bridge (again?) or as it is also called, "The Middle Eight" or there can be an Instrumental Part or maybe an Improvised Solo...

I consider the British term for this part of a song – "middle eight" – to be the best name of the bunch. In America it is more often called "the bridge", but I find this strange and confusing. As previously argued, I think the "bridge" is a name better suited for a part placed between verse and chorus. But for that we have chosen to use "pre-chorus". Phew! All these terms! Never mind that now, let us move on and decide to use the term "middle eight". "Eight" is of course referring to this part often having the length of eight bars (or measures), four beats to each measure. This is by far the most common length to this part in a pop song. But nowadays the term "middle eight" has got a broader meaning and is simply a referral to a C-part of a song, most often placed after the second chorus. It can be either vocal or instrumental. Perhaps excluded from the term is the improvised solo.

A solo will only ever be referred to as a "solo". Important: A middle eight, despite its name, must not be eight measures or bars long.

The purpose of the middle eight is to alter and differ from anything you have heard previously in the song, and of course compliment it. It wakes the listener up, gives needed pause from the established structures, renews and refreshes interest and builds anticipation for the return of the last chorus. If it is instrumental, it gives pause and respite from the vocals altogether and makes the listener long for and anticipate their return. Exactly how different to make this part is not really possible to generalize. But here is the part of a song where it is absolutely possible to get extra creative. To allow yourself to go nuts. To "let your hair down". You don't have to, of course. And most often in the name of good taste, you likely shouldn't. But you can.

Paul Simon almost made this process into an exercise of sorts, in his brilliant song "Still Crazy After All These Years". He himself tells the story in the interview book "Songwriters On Songwriting" by Paul Zollo, and if I remember it correctly it went something like this: he took only those notes *not* used so far in the song, and used them to dictate what the melody and the chords for the middle eight should be (this particular middle eight is also not eight, but sixteen, bars long). Another clear example is the Lionel Ritchie hit song "Say You, Say Me" from 1986. Here we go off into what seems like a whole new song in the middle eight. Is it fantastically smart and genius? Or is it just simply terribly bad? The jury is still out.

Have a look at it with these glasses and a listen with those ears on and judge for yourself.

If, for a middle eight, one chooses to have an improvised solo, the chords from a previous part are most often used. This is probably to try to get the best of both worlds, both having a musical foundation that the listener is already invested in, but now with the fresh take on it that the soloing on top of it offers. Of course there are, as there always are, plenty of exemptions to this "rule" of soloing over previous chord changes.

You can naturally, make the improvised solo over an entirely new part of the song.

This path, having a whole new set of chords, is more common though when there is a written instrumental part and not an improvised solo.

Also notable are the dynamics of the middle eight. They could go either way, up or down, or stay the same. Don't miss out on actively reflecting on it. Often I think it is a good idea to seize the opportunity, to change not just the chord changes, but also the dynamics when you have the chance with the middle eight, but sometimes just changing the harmonic content is enough. Let's not forget the groove. It is also a possible factor for change.

Quite often the middle eight is the point where we build a kind of pre-climax of the song. An emotional peak resulting in you having to go all in for the chorus following it. To add both intensity and a feeling of change when the chorus comes back in, a weapon at hand is to key transpose, modulating up, usually a half or a whole step. You can also choose completely the other route by breaking down the chorus after the middle eight, starting over from almost zero in terms of dynamics and intensity, providing you with the possibility of great impact when you turn it up again and bring the chorus back in, crashing like a tsunami (best case scenario, this is.)

When the chorus comes back crashing in is another common place to key transpose going up a half or a whole step.

I must admit that I hesitate whenever I make a reference to The Beatles, but man, it is hard not to. The hesitation is because it feels like not only stating the obvious but *overstating* the obvious. They were masters of just about every aspect of songwriting, while pushing the envelope and creating new forms of musical and sound expression along the way.

All of that in just 7 years of recording and before any of them had turned 30. That is pretty crazy. And makes it hard not to refer to their work from time to time in these pages...But as one of my dearest musician friends, himself a big Beatles fan says:

"We have to stop talking about The Beatles! Yes, they were the greatest, we all know that! We all agree! But come on! It has been 60 years!! WE HAVE TO MOVE ON!!"

He's got a point. It is hard to deny. In the name of progress and moving forward we will have to stop constantly referencing The Beatles at some point.

But today is not that day.

So here are just a few examples of brilliant Beatles middle eights:

Here Comes The Sun: Are you kidding me? In a cheerful pop song they throw in odd meters in an awesomely unique arrangement!

We Can Work It Out: Going first to minor and then briefly into a waltz? Genius!

Something: Groove changes. Cool arrangement and riffing. Great lyrics.

I could go on, but I will force myself to stop there. (Here, There And Everywhere) Let's get back on track:

There is of course also the possibility at this point of a kind of double whammy: To have first a vocal middle eight AND then a solo! Because sometimes, as my dear fellow Swede, Mr. Yngwie J. Malmsteen often say:
More is more!
If you do have first a vocal middle eight AND then a solo, you might need to watch out though, for any of these effects:

#It might be too much and too long and overblown and over-the-top, making the listener tune out. Or maybe it's just right! Try!

#If you use the chorus chords for the solo, make sure there is enough change potential left when the vocals come back in to make it lift.

#Make sure that the dramatic structure works. Try to make sure that the energy "travels" properly through the song. Where is the peak? Is there more than one peak? Is there headroom left to raise the intensity enough to make the last chorus or the parts after the solo to keep the interest of the listener?

Let's move forward to:

The Last Chorus

So, now we have made it this far. The last chorus of the song.
The looming question being: What do we want to do now? Where do we go with the last chorus, and what do we do with it to make it everything both we and the listener want it to be, and hopefully even more?
How do we "drive it home"? Make it feel complete and satisfying? How we accomplish that, obviously depends on where we are coming from and what kind of song we are writing.

Are not the choices quite simply these: more of the same, or change? Your song might be a simple ABABB, and in this case we have come to the last BB. A double chorus and then the end. Nothing more to it.
Or, we change it up in some way. We might up the dynamics to the max (more performance and production than songwriting though). We might break it down and then build it back up to the max. We might key transpose for intensity.
Sometimes substitute a chord or two.

When we break it down and then pick it back up, a little trick is to start from the top of the chorus when the full intensity comes back in, even if we were halfway though it already in the breakdown. Very common is to have a double chorus or more at the end of a chorus song, to make sure we squeeze out every possible drop of juice from the song.

The B Chorus
(Can also be called Complement Chorus or Alternative Chorus)

This is a not so common puppy. Still, I thought it was worth mentioning. Although it has shown its face earlier in pop history, it has been made popular (or perhaps maybe it just trended briefly in the late nineties) by Max Martin. The B chorus is primarily inserted after the middle eight, often uses the lyrics of the regular chorus (or slightly varied) but with a new melody, creating a moment of suspense before it transitions back to the regular chorus

Example:
I Want It That Way - Backstreet Boys
Opps!... I Did It Again – Britney Spears.

The Outro

An outro can be the same thing as the last chorus or choruses, and only using this name to describe where we are in the song.

The most common choice is to let the choruses roll on for a third or a fourth time while perhaps changing up the vocals. Sometimes the backup vocal part changes, freeing up the lead vocals to go on a wailing excursion. Often a lead instrument comes in and takes over. But an outro can also be a whole new separate part. This feature is not that commonplace in pop, but it is definitely worth mentioning.

Examples:
Rosanna - Toto
Don't Give Up - Peter Gabriel
Hey Jude - The Beatles
Fix You -Coldplay
Layla -Derek and The Dominos
The Chain -Fleetwood Mac
On Every Street -Dire Straits

The Ending

There are in a sense really only two or three different ways to end a song. Either you have a written and arranged ending, which might just mean ending on the root chord on "the one" (the first beat of a bar, that is), or using a more sophisticated tie- it-all-together ending riff.

Caveat no 8575664839:

Although it is the most common practice to the end on the root chord of the key you are in, you don't have to do so. The reason for ending on the root chord, most would probably agree, is the feeling it brings of "coming home". Of resolution. Release. Landing. Finish.

If you end on any other chord, there will be a different feel.

Example no 1: I "Take It Easy" – The Eagles

"Take It Easy" is mainly a feel good up tempo Country soft rock tune in G major. Although the chorus shifts to the relative E minor and the outro turns into G mixolydian (that can, oversimplified, be explained as using the chords from C major but with G major as root). Then it goes and ends on E minor. Why?

I don't have the faintest clue. They just thought it sounded cool, probably. Which is of course, a perfectly good reason. I don't really get why it should end on a minor chord though, and I have heard more than one colleague state derogatory opinions about it. This still doesn't mean that it is bad, obviously.

> “Opinions are like assholes, everybody’s got one”
>
> — *Dirty Harry*

Example no 2: "Against All Odds (Take A Look At Me Now)" – Phil Collins

This lovely song ends on the dominant or V chord, leaving an unresolved feeling

Example no 3: "Betty" – Taylor Swift

Ends on a IV chord or the sub-dominant. Also an unresolved feeling. Like everything is "still up in the air".

So as you can see by these different choices: you can either end on the root or tonic or 1 chord (same thing), for an obvious and easy feel of finishing, Or you can end on another chord lending the ending different degrees of an unfinished feeling, depending on what other chord you choose.
Or you end on another chord lending the ending different degrees of an unfinished feeling, depending on what other chord you choose.

If you do end on the tonic chord, but still want it to be more jazzy, you can colour it to taste. It is a chapter in and of it self to list different ways to colour an end chord in a jazzy way, so if you want that, just pick up a few and add them to your vocabulary.

Or, what the heck, here are a few of my favs (the root of A is of course random):

A9b5add13: A-Eb-G-C#-F#-B

A6/g:A-C#-E-F#-B

Or like I said before, you can also end a song with an arranged little riff thing.

Examples:

"Smoke On The Water" – Deep Purple
"Holy Diver" – Dio
"Twist and Shout" – The Beatles

Another completely different way to end a song is of course the classic fade out.

The fade out ending can sometimes though feel like a bit of a cop out. It can be seen as a bit lazy. I have heard it be viewed as if it is saying "I am not engaged enough in this song to bother with writing a proper ending for it". However, in periods from the 50s and forward on through the 80s it was an immensely popular way to end a song.

The idea of it at all being the "lazy" solution can surely be argued. For starters, it can of course be an artistically active choice. It could be that a fade-out ending is what you truly hear in your mind for your song. And in that case, no one can really argue your right to such an ending, and that would kind of close the book on that matter. The fade-out might also have a psychological effect that you could find desirable.

When a song doesn't have a "proper" ending, it reaches no conclusion. The music the remains as an open loop that the unconscious keeps playing over and over, forever seeking conclusion.

Sidenote:
Here is a recording tip on another type of fade, that is the last ringing chord of your song: This might sound trivial but it is NOT! When recording, always, always, always, when hitting that last chord or note or cymbal, let it ring for as long as possible. At least for a slow count to seven. If I had a penny or a nickel or a dime or a small amount of money, for each time I have had to time stretch or cut paste to get a decent fade just because the musicians were impatient and eager to say something either good or bad about the take just made.

And I am absolutely saying that also top-class musicians can let this slip their minds. (Not Grammy winning producer/arranger Mattias Bylund though. Ever.) So, remember this:

Hold
That
Chord
And/Or
Wait
For
That
Cymbal
To
Ring
Out
For
A
Count
Of
Seven
Or
So
God
Damnit!

The Cookie

A whole other song structure than what is presented above is a structure sometimes referred to as a "Cookie"

A Cookie is when you don't have a verse/chorus situation but just a verse, that often ends with the title of the song being kind of a conclusion of the story in the verse.

Example:

"The Times They Are A-Changing" . Bob Dylan

An often used structure in a Cookie is to have a B part, not as a chorus, but just slightly different chords and melody. Sometimes represented more than once in the song. For example, like this

AABABA

Example:

"You're Gonna Make Me Lonesome When You Go" – Bob Dylan

Starting A New Song

> "I don't force it. If you don't have an idea and you don't hear anything going over and over in your head, don't sit down and try write a song. You know, go mow the lawn... My songs speak for themselves."
>
> — *Neil Young*

> "I am a professional songwriter. I don't wait for inspiration. I start writing a song as soon as the phone call comes commissioning a tune."
>
> — *Sammy Cahn*

These above statements come from two songwriting legends with absolute polarized views on writing. But there ya go. Different strokes for different folks. When you start writing a new song there are only a few places you can be in. Firstly, either you have an idea for the new song, or you don't.

But also, the incitement for writing a song can be either your own, as in writing a song just because you feel like writing a song, or the incitement may be that you have received a request of some kind to write a song. There are, I believe, quite different ways to handle these different starting points. And I now feel that we might need to try and make these "categories" a bit clearer.

The different starting points might be categorized as follows:

1. Needing/wanting to write a song, but you start from scratch without any previous idea for the piece whatsoever
2. Needing/wanting to write a song for yourself, from an existing idea.
3. Needing/wanting to write a commissioned song to a brief that contains direction.

Let's start with No.1. The starting point where you want to write a song for no special reason other than "just because", but having no prior musical or lyrical idea for it.

Let's change the name of this chapter to:

Starting A New Song Fresh, But Having No Idea Where To Start
(or Having no ideas, but how to go looking for an idea about an idea!)

Why not do just that very thing we are talking about and run down the process in real time right now? Let's write a song right now from scratch. As of this moment I don't have an idea for a song. But maybe I can find an idea for an idea? The circumstances are very much ideal for this exercise, aren't they!?

No matter how much I or anyone else talks about songwriting, when push comes to shove, you have to do the heavy lifting yourself. You will have to go out on your own. Stop! Wait! Back up a bit... I like that!

Go Out On Your Own

Doesn't that have a ring to it?

I like it! And after just test-singing these words for a while and trying chords with the spontaneous, simple, but somewhat nice little melody that showed up, I now find myself with this:

You got to Go Out On You Own
Go Out On Your Own
Find out for yourself, turning every stone
Go Out On Your Own

As every line ends with a rhyme for "own", this gives us the following rhyming scheme:

A

A

A

A

A

Every line rhymes, since the only word that is not "own" is the perfect rhyme "stone". Extremely simplistic, even naive if you will. But in this case I like it.

I like to keep a rhyme dictionary at hand when writing. Nowadays it is most often an online version like rhymezone.com. And picking good ones that rhyme for "own" gives me this short list:

Own
Alone
Bone
Cone
Phone
Prone
Stone
Zone

That gives us alternatives for that third line in the middle. I feel it might be nice if that line is different for every chorus, so I will come back to that later, but for now I am going with:

Find out for yourself, Turn every stone

There is a slight temporal problem here though.

For it to be perfect it should be:

Find out for yourself, Turn every stone

The initial version has a ring to it though.

Find out for yourself, Turning every stone

As in: You find out for yourself while you are out there turning every stone. And that all of those extra context giving words are self-explanatory. We'll see what version to keep.

But I'll keep it for now. This is our chorus. As I say elsewhere somewhere within the pages of this humble book, I prefer to start with the chorus for a reason. Let's recap that. When, like now, I have started with the chorus, all I need to do is to come up with a story of how I got there. To the place where the person in the chorus is, that is. It can be any story. The road lies open. And that thought, the feeling and the vision of endless possibilities being just like an an open road, before us is a very appealing one to me. Also, singing this, it is naturally starting to take the form of some kind of a waltz. A 3/4 or 6/8 time.

So, what can I write about here? Let's see what we have so far...

You got to Go Out On You Own
Go Out On Your Own
Find out for yourself

Turn every stone
You got to Go Out On You Own
Go Out On Your Own

It sounds to me like I am giving somebody some kind of advice, doesn't it? Let's try moving forward with that "advice giving" thought.

Advice, advice
To add sugar or add spice

This line just popped into my head "for free"..
If it hadn't, I would have made a short list of rhymes for "advice")
Let's move on

Advice, advice
To add sugar or add spice
If I only had some to give
But I'm not a wise man
Hardly even a nice man
And can't provide a blueprint
For how life should be lived

The rest of that bit also just showed up. To me that ow means I am on to something.

The melody notes that come spontaneously with the words, lend themselves to a pretty but somewhat mundane cadence of descending diatonic chords in D-major.

The chord progression is **D A/C# Bm A G A D**

Nothing wrong with that progression AT ALL. But I will try to spice it up with colorations that fits the melody, just because I feel like it. This may arguably steer of a little bit from songwriting and into arranging in some peoples view, but for it helps to set the mood and that in turn might help drive the songwriting process. So now the chord progression is:

D Fm#/C# Bm7 D/A G A6 D

That is the first half of the verse. The second half now is:

D Fm#/C# Bm7 D/A G A6 F#7sus F#7

Let us call that a verse and tie it to the chorus.

Advice, advice
To add sugar or add spice
If I only had some to give
But I'm not a wise man
Hardly even a nice man
And can't provide a blueprint
For how life should be lived

You got to Go Out On You Own
Go Out On Your Own
Find out for yourself
Turn every stone
You got to Go Out On You Own

Go Out On Your Own

The chord sequence I am liking for the chorus is this:

G6 A6 D G6 A6 D
G6 A6 D G6 A6 D
G6 A6 D F#7 Bm7
G6 A6 Bm7 G6 A6 D

Now the story is starting to feel a bit like a parent speaking to a child. Having three kids of my own, I can very much relate, and I think I like it! Let us roll with this idea and see where it goes.

This new parent sending his child-out-into-the-world-with-some-advice idea helps me with the second verse. Second verses can sometimes be a bit tricky I feel, but I think I am cracking a nut here as to what this song might be about and for.

With this topic I can now draw from my own life. As I am writing this, my middle child is turning nineteen. This song will not be autobiographical, not exactly about neither her nor me specifically, but rather an abstraction of both our personalities and our situation.
The idea of drawing from these actual feelings gives me much needed perspective on how to continue this song. Suddenly the direction of the song has become much clearer.

After some noodling and humming I get this for the second verse:

To play the all-knowing father
Well, I won't even bother
To pretend that I've got but a clue

To go left or go right
To run or to fight
And if you stumble 'pon the answer
Please enlighten this old chancer
Of what and of what not to do

And that's right. If anyone noticed, I veered off the path here and left the format from verse 1 just a little, by repeating and adding an extra phrase:

And if you stumble 'pon the answer
Please enlighten this old chancer
Of what and of what not to do

I liked the idea since it offers a bit of variety and may help to wake up the listener's ear just a tad, the idea being that the ear with take for granted that the form will be the same as the last verse, and then it is not. Plus, I think the lyrics have some charm to them.

So now the song is starting to take form! Let's review what we have so far:

Advice, advice
To add sugar or spice
If I only had some to give
But I'm not a wise man
Hardly even a nice man
And can't provide a blueprint
For how life should be lived

You got to Go Out On Your Own
Go Out On Your Own
Find out for yourself
Turn every stone
You got to Go Out On Your Own
Go Out On Your Own

To play the all-knowing father
Well, I won't even bother
To pretend that I've got but a clue
To go left or go right
To run or to fight
And if you stumble 'pon the answer
Please enlighten this old chancer
Of what and of what not to do

You got to Go Out On Your Own
Go Out On Your Own
Find out for yourself/ See the world yourself
Turn every stone/Be a rolling stone
You got to Go Out On Your Own
Go Out On Your Own

The third and fourth phrase of the chorus offers a possibility of being changed up. That's why I put both options in there. My idea is that you can switch these lines for new ones every chorus. As long as they rhyme with "own" and that these new lines make sense in the narrative. My only concern is that "see the world yourself" is perhaps a bit pompous and "be a rolling stone" a bit... I dunno... cliché? Hmmm... I'll have to sleep on that one...

I also think that this tune should start straight into the first line of the verse. No intro. Like "Hey Jude" or "The Long And Winding Road".
(I forgot we were supposed to try and stop referencing The Beatles!)

Not to jump lightyears ahead in the process, but worth mentioning:

Starting a song off with immediate "content" instead of with an intro that makes you wait and build the anticipation, can give you what radio people often refer to as "starters". That means a song they can hand the "relay baton" right over to and off it goes.

Double caveat: When this book comes out, there might not be "radio" anymore anyway. I am old and it is a thing of the past. To all you young people: Google it. It used to be big.

This business of having an intro or having no intro is of course debatable, as to whether or not that is an integral part of the song or merely part of the arrangement.

And while on that topic....

What *is* really the *song* and what *is* instead the *arrangement*? It is not an easy or self-evident question. It is also not a question we can hope to "solve" here and now. But I will try to present at least a vague definition:
I would venture to say that the song, most of the time, is the lyrics and the melody. Not the chords. Not the groove. Nothing more than the lyrics and the melody.
Most of the time.

There are of course, as always exceptions.

For example, what in Frank Zappa's "Inca Roads" is the song and what is the arrangement? What is Smoke On The Water without the guitar riff?

Actually, I realize that I have heard a Bossa Nova version of Smoke On The Water that didn't include the riff in any form or shape. And it was still Smoke On The Water.

There are of course thousands of songs, tunes and pieces of music like this where it is unclear what to name as the song and what to call merely a part of the arrangement.

I will return to this subject in a later chapter, further trying to define what a song is from the perspective of "song or performance piece", but for now let's leave this and go back to writing this parental advice song we were working on..

So where were we...

Oh yes, we started directly with the verse. We then did verse-chorus-verse- chorus (ABAB), but now what? This is a classic sticking point. Let's review our options.

#1. Just another chorus or double chorus, then straight to the end

#2. C-part with lyrics (sometimes called middle eight or bridge)

#3. Improvised instrumental solo

#4. Instrumental C-part

Option 1 is too plain and dull for this particular song, I think. Sometimes for a real folky song, keeping it that plain and simple is absolutely the way to go. But for this... I am just feeling... no.

Option 2... Hmm... this is also a no go. The tune is already "wordy", meaning it is lyric driven. There is a lot of words. So maybe now, less is more. That is: no more lyrics. Enough words already!
Or maybe this is just me being lazy. Because I know that any additional words now would have to be the best and strongest ones in the song to cut it. Only if the new words I would add at this point are as good as, or preferably better than what has come before, will they add and not subtract and dilute.

Maybe I'm just being too lazy to work hard enough to find them. I don't know.

Option 3. Maybe. But no. I'm not really feeling an improvised ego spotlighting solo on here. Perhaps a nice John Mayer-esque solo can work... but no...

Option 4. Yes. I think so. An Instrumental C-Part! This is what I am feeling... The idea that comes to mind, is to write an instrumental C-part that is almost... "over the top"... Maybe a key change... a new melody theme played by strings and horns and bells and whistles. I am thinking that the song starts very plainly instrumentation- wise. Just piano and voice.

(I know this is more arrangement than song, but these pictures in my head are also part of my process, so shoot me!).

The instrumentation then stays pretty sparse all the way up to here, maybe adding something along the way. A bass, maybe some guitar... I haven't decided about drums yet. It should be sparse, though, until this C-part. The part should symbolize the young person going off discovering both the world and even life itself. Overly sentimental you say? Pretentious? YES! You bet! But sometimes being pretentious is fun, and sometimes more is absolutely more!

There is an old Swedish word for this. pekoral It doesn't seem to exist in English, so I am introducing it to the English language, right here and now. (I must do everything I can to make this an incredibly important and groundbreaking book!)

This is the definition of the word in Swedish from Wikipedia:

"A text written in a grandiloquent or pompous style but lacking literary quality, thus making it seem overly pretentious or ridiculous."

I would argue though, that contrary to the Wiki definition, it need not be just text. It can be used to describe the intent or the execution of any expressive idea.

So it is decided. I will risk make this instrumental part into a pekoral.

And it will risk being pekoral by choice. Think Nat King Cole or Sinatra type arrangements by Nelson Riddle. Not that those excellent artists and others of that style and their arrangements are pekoral per se, it has of course to do with the context and situation. I just get the feeling that me going overboard with this in this song, for this artistic reason, might walk that razors edge of being overly pompous and a pekoral. And I love the thought!

That being said: I am of course hoping to "pull it off", that is that it will feel in place and motivated. But I am going "all in"...
For this Instrumental interlude I feel like doing a key transpose to really mark the spot.

A trick that comes to mind is this:

Since we are repeatedly coming 4-5-1 in the chorus, I will now swap the last Tonic, the Root or the 1 chord for a new tonic. The key I am working in for the moment, I don't know if this key will be changed later, is D major.

That makes 4=G to 5=A to 1=D

The new key I am transposing to is Bb major. So in the last phrase of the chorus we go

G A Bb (instead of going to D)

Why the key change from D major to Bb major works in this case, is because of the vocal melody. The last note of the melody goes to the tonic note D, and normally the song goes to full harmonic resolution with the tonic chord D major. But when I substitute the D major for a Bb major, the D note in the melody relates well to the Bb major also, since the note D is the major third of the Bb major chord. This common note will make the key transpose work.

Now we have transitioned into Bb major and for this part I am thinking classic American songbook chord changes. They will not be hard to come up with since I have written dozens of songs in that style and have studied these chord changes a lot.

The bigger challenge will be how to neatly and musically transpose back at the end of the C-part interlude and come as seamlessly back to the original key to go into the last chorus. Right now I only know that this is what I want to do, but not yet how to accomplish it. Give me a minute...

After a few attempts, this is what I've got:

Bbmaj Gm7 Cm7 Eb F7
Bbmaj Gm7 Cm7 Bb/D
Eb/G# Eb/F F#7sus F#7

Then we are back to the chorus

G A D

So now we have our C-part. An instrumental interlude that will be arranged to appear big and bold. Over the top.

And I've actually also found a pretty good artistic excuse for doing so!
Since the song is about coming of age, about an adolescent going oI out into the world on his or her own, this instrumental part is the going out into the world, and because the world is big and overwhelming, so is the music portraying it! Good excuse, yes?
We now have this: A B A B C

But, the end and transition and transpose back to the last chorus is NOT up to par...

I have an idea for a solution though. If I instead of the F#7sus go to a G7sus it sound smoother and we will have transposed to Eb coming back to the last chorus. This might be beneficial, being that it might help by bringing up the intensity and carry us in style the last bit of the song. But I would rather be in the key of E, just because it is an easier key to handle, and I am lazy. So, I tried and added another transition in.
I go G7sus-G7 to G#7sus-G#7

So now we have:

Bbmaj Gm7 Cm7 Eb F7
Bbmaj Gm7 Cm7 Bb/D
Eb/G# Eb/F G7sus G7 G#7sus G#7

And then we find ourselves in the key of E with the chords of the chorus now instead being:

A6 B6 E A6 B6 E
A6 B6 E A6 B6 E
A6 B6 E G#7 Cm7
A6 B6 C#m7 A6 B6 E

I'm thinking this will help give the last choruses after this intense instrumental a well- deserved bump in urgency and energy.
I also think there will be a short breakdown to a soft chorus. It will make for a re-boot of the dynamics, giving both me and the listener a quick breather, giving us the potential and the chance to pick it back up again from zero to full intensity, have the band go full throttle, have the strings come back in and join for the last double chorus, and then it's The End.
So, the whole shebang looks like this, top to bottom:

Go Out On Your Own

Advice, advice
To add sugar or spice
If I only had some to give
But I'm not a wise man
Hardly even a nice man
And can't provide a blueprint
For how life should be lived

You got to Go Out On Your Own
Go Out On Your Own
Find out for yourself
Turn every stone
You got to Go Out On Your Own
Go Out On Your Own

To play the all-knowing father
Well, I won't even bother
To pretend that I've got but a clue
To go left or go right
To run or to fight
And if you stumble 'pon the answer
Please enlighten this old chancer
Of what and of what not to do

You got to Go Out On Your Own
Go Out On Your Own
Find out for yourself
Be a rolling stone
You got to Go Out On Your Own
Go Out On Your Own

You got to Go Out On Your Own
Go Out On Your Own
See the world yourself
But then you come back home
You got to Go Out On Your Own
Go Out On Your Own
You got to Go Out On Your Own

There it is. Actually pretty good. I like it. A few more thoughts on the piece:

Again, the reason for modulating (changing the key) to E-major instead of D-major, when going from the Instrumental Interlude to the last chorus is to bring the vocals up in register a little bit to try to gain more intensity.

This is to better match the energy we have picked up in the instrumental part and be able to drive this tune home energy wise without it losing wind on the finish line. Also, the previously discussed lines 3 and 4 again get switched for new ones but not only that, they have now also been doubled. That left me with a few choices of chords with those repeated lines. The basic chords would be IV-V-I (4-5-1) and in the key of E-major that means A-B-E. But since going to the E gives us a feeling of resolve, like we've come home, and we want to postpone that, hold it off a little, I change the E to its relative minor C#m. But to add a little further tension before the release, I use a common old jazz trick and change that relative minor to a dominant 7. I also put the sus4 and the release of the sus4 in there.

So, C#m becomes C#7sus and C#7.

Except for the second repeat, when the last word is "alone" – then I go with C#m. Both because it offers variation, but also because it is a better match for that ending word with its slightly sad or blue feel. Lastly, I do the same thing harmonically as when we went into the Instrumental C-part. In this new key of E that means going from A to B and then landing on a Cmajor7. Then I wanted the classic ending of making the IV chord (subdominant) into a minor chord, before resolving to the I chord (root). In the key of E this would mean A-minor to E.

Go Out On Your Own

Martin Carlberg

32 G A D Em7 F#m7 G A
Go out on your own Find out for yourself And
35 F#7 Bm G A Bm
be a rolling stone You gotta go out on your own
38 G A Bb6 Gm7 Cm7 Bb/D
Go out on your own
42 F(sus4) F Bb6 Gm Gm7/F Cm7 Bb/D
46 G# Bb(sus4)/F G7(sus4) G7
49 G#7(sus4) G#7 A B E E Fm G#m
You got to Go out on your own
53 A B E A B
Go out on your own Find out for yourself Be
56 G#7 C#m A B C#m
a rolling stone Go out on your own
59 A B F#7 C#m
Go out on your own
61 A B C6 E E
Go out on your own

But, a problem: The melody carried over from before that I don't feel like changing (although of course you CAN), suggests that I would then sing the note A accompanied by the chord A-minor.

Since we are at some kind of dramatic point of climax, this will be harmonically bland and will not suffice. So, let's use another little jazz trick. This chord when used like this with this function, as a minor substitution for the subdominant (A-minor instead of A-major in the key of E in this case), can be moved around in minor thirds just like a diminished chord. It goes over even more smoothly if we give it some more harmonic information. So instead of A-minor we move it up a minor third to C-minor. Then I add the intervals 6 and 9 for good measure and good fun.

So that gives us this ending of the song:

A B Cmaj7 Cm69 Emaj7

P.S. I changed and changed the last lines again and again... But kept the above text (plus this) to show that this changing and changing a thousand times over can and does happen. The final choice is what you hear on the recording.

(Even that is not for certain ...I might change it again before then)

"I think songwriting is the ultimate form of being able to make anything that happens in your life productive."

— *Taylor Swift*

MODULATING KEY

Since this song, "Go Out Of Your Own Way", contained a key modulation, I thought it might be appropriate to throw in a brief section about this musical finesse.

The argument could be made that key modulation is an arrangement thing and not a songwriting thing. And while this sometimes probably could be true, a lot of the times, key changes are an absolute part of the song.

There could be a million and reasons that I can think of for wanting to change the key of a song (means the same thing as modulating) inside the song. A very common reason is to raise the key by one or two semitones for the last chorus to make the vocalists range sound a bit more pressured and hopefully thereby, more urgent. By this we are amping up the energy for the finale of the song and making sure we max it out. Another reason is that it adds to the harmonic movement of the song to modulate between different parts of a song. It challenges the ear and refreshes the interest of the listener. At best. But it can also if done less than well, create harmonic confusion and work to the opposite end, and instead throw the ear of the listener off track.

There are a few different ways to modulate keys. Since I am not the most educated and theoretical songwriter, I only know of the following the methods. I am sure there are more. But these three will go a long way.

The first way is the simplest. Let's call it:

Direct Modulation

This means what it says and says what it means. You just start a new part of a song in a new key.
Since this absolutely throws the ear of the listener off, it needs to be used with a great deal of finesse. Or brute force. Sometimes conviction is the way to sell such a move.

Example:
If I Ever Lose My Faith In You -Sting
Think - Aretha Franklin
Hungry Heart -Bruce Springsteen (Going into the solo)

Common Tone Modulation

The modulation in "Go Out On Your Own" was an example of common tone modulation. The song played in the key of G Major and at the end of the second chorus we were coming from the dominant chord in G Major which is D Major, heading for the expected resolve of the tonic chord G Major. The melody on the resolving tonic chord was also the root note G. Maximum resolve, that is. But instead of the G Major I instead go to the new tonic of Bb Major. The

G note now has the harmonic interval of a major sixth. To help sell this to the listener I make it a Bb6, but this is optional and not really necessary. There were indeed other options available than Bb. C# Major, for instance. This would make the melody note G into the major third if C# Major. Or if we just go up a semitone to G# Major and make the first tonic of the modulation a G# major 7 to make the sale. This, since the melody note G is the major seventh of G# Major.

Example: Penny Lane -The Beatles

New Dominant Modulation

This simply means that you "signal" or more appropriately put, lead into the new key, by playing the dominant chord of the new key that you are modulation to, just before you play the tonic of the new key. Like for instance if we are in the key of C Major and want to change the key to D Major. Imagine that we have an G Major chord (the dominant chord of C Major) at the end of the chord progression right before we go to the top again. Either you flat out change that G Major to a A Major, or you split the measure and go G to A, or you let it land on the C tonic and then throw in the A. Point is, as soon as you play that A, you are creating an expectancy of resolution to D Major and not C Major.

Example: Hungry Heart -Bruce Springsteen (Coming back from the solo)

STARTING A NEW SONG, SCENARIO NO 2

This chapter will address the starting point of needing or wanting to write a song, but from an already existing idea. Now, this could still mean that we are writing this song for ourselves, for no special reason other than "just because", but this time we have an idea to start from, or it can also mean that we might have a request for a song, and we think this idea that we already had floating around in the ether of our creative mind, might work for it.

An idea for a song can be anything really. A riff, a fragment of a melody, a few chords that go together in a way we like. It could be groove, maybe or a bass line. It can of course be a lyrical idea that you want to start writing from, but I thought that was worthy of its own chapter later on.

Let's follow one or two of these: "Riff", "Music", "lyrics", "Groove", "Bass line" – as if they were the starting point of our writing process one at a time, shall we? I don´t know yet which of these I will pick to go with, but let´s start with:

The Riff

So, you have this cool riff. Then you might want to ask

yourself, where does it lead? Where does it want to go? What would be satisfying for YOU to hear after the riff? What would you like to hear once you have heard this riff enough times?

One common practice is to go the other way. Since a riff is by definition information rich, then perhaps just chugging on a chord? Long chords? Or instead go to yet another riff? I think it is good to learn a lot of songs, and I do mean a LOT of songs. This gives you a vast library, a bank of knowledge if you will, of what the history of song making has gone before in similar situations. And then choose to go either with or against the choices previously used by others.

Stacking riffs after each other can be interesting, but also feel a bit stifled, as if it is treading water and there is no real release. A good reference though of when this works is Metallica and many others in the Metal genre where it is common to stack riffs on top of each other.

One way to go is to decide what function the riff has.

In our standing example Deep Purple's "Smoke On The Water" for instance, the riff is as we have mentioned, a kind of hook that ties everything in the song together. In addition to having this magnificent riff, in fact one of the most significant guitar riffs of all time, this tune has got even more to offer. The legend says Ritchie Blackmore was inspired by Beethoven's 5th Symphony played backwards when he came up with the riff.

He then went from the riff into a verse with simple chords (G and F), but then into a chorus with the interesting and unusual chords (for a song in the key of G minor) C- G#. Or to be exact, it is the G# that is the interesting and uncommon choice for a song in G minor. I can oIer no technical explanation why this works.

The only explanation is: **it sounds cool!!!**

And that is the only explanation really needed!

This is the song structure for "Smoke On The Water"

Riff
Verse
Chorus
Riff
Verse
Chorus
Riff
Solo
Riff

In Van Halen's "Panama" we also start off with a riff. This riff never returns in the song. We then go into another little riff. This riff in the same way does not return later in the song. We then go into a third riff that is later also used in the chorus.

The same band had of course a monster hit with the song

“Jump”. Here the riff is keyboard-based and is used for the intro and then the chorus.

So why not write us a riff based song right now.

I will use a really simple funky blues riff that has been showing up lately whenever I pick up a guitar. I will then take that riff and throw myself down a creative flight of stairs and hope that I land on my feet. I had better... Wait... That ain’t too bad!

"Throw myself down a creative flight of stairs and hope that I land on my feet".

Land On My Feet...
I don’t yet know why, but i like this.

Land on my feet is now the working title of this tune.

The riff I have come up with, by itself I realize, is nothing much. I beg your pardon for this. But if played right I think it can be groovy. I must say that I feel a “Performance Piece” in the making. What I mean by that I will explain later, but this tune will work also as an example of that. It might actually be lazy to use this riff. Maybe I should work harder at being inventive. But for this exercise, the process is more important than the ideas themselves being of re-inventing the wheel quality. So let us see if we can make a hen out of this feather. Make a soup from a rusty nail.

Back to the work at hand.

I feel like this riff serves as both intro and verse.

Since it feels like a bluesy thang of a tune, the lyrics should be accordingly stylistically appropriate.

After a bit of singing and riffing I seem to have made it into a "Cookie", meaning that there is no verse-chorus but each verse ends with the title of the song as a conclusion.
Here we go. Blues style genre lyric writing:

Well Baby I've been wronged
I've been made a fool
For much too long
No more than your tool

I've been put down
I've been thrown out on the street
But baby baby
I'm gonna Land On My Feet
You can rest assured baby
I'm gonna Land On My Feet

So, thus far, the minimalistic riff is basically the foundation for the whole song.

It serves as both intro and verse. The only elements adding harmonic information are the chords under the title.
The format is similar to a 12-bar blues, but since we repeat the title tagline it becomes a 16-bar blues.

For what is known as the "Turnaround" that goes V-IV-I, I

want there to be a little specific thing on the IV chord, and that is simply to first play the third of the IV in the bass and then the root of the IV before going to the I chord. Again this might be seen as more of arrangement thing though, than what constitutes as the actual song.

It looks like we might play this in the key of A, for no other reason than it suits my voice when I sing this. What we have now is this simple 16-bar chord progression:

A A A A A A A A A A E D/F# D A A E D/F#D A A

Arrangement wise we now have

A= Riff
B=verse

Even though they are almost the same.

I will not fight the feeling that we simply must go around the same form once more. This is more of a song where we use and play with clichés, than one were we are daring and inventive.

Remember the "Bernstein Principle":

1. Introduce
2. Establish
3. Alter

So after another riff, let's try coming up with another verse and make it: A B A B

For verse 2 I will only be continuing this rather unremarkable story of this wronged and a bit whiny person:

You know I stumbled
And then I fell
My whole world crumbled
It was a living hell
Might think I'd be broken
From your words so mean
But baby baby
I'm gonna Land On My Feet
You can rest assured baby
I'm gonna Land On My Feet

The genre definitely calls for a solo now so let's do that. I feel it needs to be on the same vamp, so:

A B A B A(solo)

After that, now, what to do? This bluesy genre can often be really simple, structure wise, so we could just wrap it up with another verse and then the end or more solo and then go to the end. But I am going to try to put in a C-part. And I am going to try a favourite trick, which is to regard the dominant feeling of everything we have had in the chords so far as "major" even though I sing and play the minor pentatonic scale over it.

A B A B A(solo) C

You know what they say
Can't keep a good man down
Gonna have to work on
Being less a clown

And then straight into one last verse:

After trying and trying again. Twisting and turning this arrangement with the C-part. I had to surrender to this "fact": The C-part didn't work, so it went out the window. I could have of course have edited this part out, but decided to keep it in since it shows the ongoing process. It is always hit and miss..

This tune will stick to the simple and road tested 16-bar blues format.

So instead of going to a c-part from the solo, we go straight back into one last verse

A B A B A(solo) B

Let's try to come up with some kind of summation of this story in a third verse:

But now I'm back
Ahead of the game
The guy you remember
Just ain't the same
Well I told you so baby

I always Land On My Feet
Did you hear me when I said
I always Land On My Feet

To round it all up, let's let the form run one more time as an outro with more solo on top. Also a few more repeats of the title never hurt anyone. A little stop thing in the end to enhance the ending and then a classic slight ritardando and then we are done.

There it is. A simple little groovy song from a simple little riff. I will do my best to perform well on it and by that breathe life into this "performance piece".

Land On My Feet

Well Baby I've been wronged
I've been made a fool
For much too long
No more than your tool
I've been put down
I've been thrown out on the street
But baby baby
I'm gonna Land On My Feet
You can rest assured baby
I'm gonna Land On My Feet

You know I stumbled
And then I fell
My whole world crumbled
It wasn't well

Might call me broken
From your words so mean
But baby baby
I'm gonna Land On My Feet
Now rest assured baby
I'm gonna Land On My Feet

But now I'm back
Ahead of the game
The guy you remember
He just ain't the same
I've got a smile
For every one I meet
And I told you so baby
I always Land On My Feet
Now, didn't you hear me when I said
I always Land On My Feet

Land On My Feet
Land On My Feet
You can sleep well knowing baby
I always Land On My Feet
You should have believed me when I told ya
I always Land On My Feet
You can rest assured knowing baby
I always Land On My Feet

Land On My Feet

M Carlberg

2
46
E7 D/F# D7 A7 E7 A7
But now I'm back Ahead of the game
52
The guy you remember He just ain't the same I've got a smile
55
For everyone I meet And I told you so baby
58
I always Land On My Feet Now didn't you hear me when I said
62
I always land on my feet
68
Land On My Feet Land On My Feet
72
You can sleep well knowing baby I always Land On My Feet
75
You should have belived me when I told ya I always Land On
79
My Feet You can rest assured knowing baby I
82
always Land On My Feet

LYRICS

"It's very helpful to start with something that's true. If you start with something that's false, you're always covering your tracks. Something simple and true, that has a lot of possibilities, is a nice way to begin."

— *Paul Simon*

Here is a really important question: What are GOOD lyrics? Why are good lyrics good? What makes them good? And what makes bad lyrics BAD? It is of course an impossible question to answer, but, for me to have something about anything to write in this chapter, let's pretend it is not. Let's go on a quest to hunt this elusive answer down.

"The melody and the chord structure comes pretty quickly, lyrics are the bitch."

— *Rufus Wainright*

I think it was Frank Zappa who said something like, "Good lyrics are simply lyrics that do what they are intended to do”. In the same breath he mentioned Da Doo Ron Ron by The Crystals as one of his favourite lyrics, which to him showcased and exemplified this rule of thumb.

I am not sure this “do what they are intended to do” idea completely entails and encompasses this matter. Well, I guess that it is sometimes true. But then other times... Can a set of lyrics not have unintended qualities? I say yes, absolutely they can.
Does even the intent of the lyrics have to be clear to the writer?

I dare say no. They do not.

A good example of that is “The Bowie Method”. Legend has it that David Bowie used to take scissors to the daily papers and cut out random words, that he then pieced together to make up lyrics that he himself had no clue to of their meaning.

Another example is from the documentary film “Imagine”, where a man has camped (or squatted really) in John Lennons garden for days and days when Lennon himself decides to go out and talk some sense into the man. The somewhat confused man recites Lennons own lyrics back to him, fills some of them with his own interpreted meaning, and asks Lennon for the meaning of other Beatles lyrics. Lennon tells him though this the man´s interpretations are not necessarily at all the meanings of the words and that, although he wrote them, Lennon himself does not know what the lyrics mean. The words were just stuff made up on the spot and top of mind.

So I feel that the Zappa quote, although it has some kind of point to it, doesn't get us that far on our journey towards the truth of the matter. What would happen if we were to modify Zappa's quote a bit?
Upgrade it...
(upgrade on a Zappa quote??? Is anyone even allowed to try????).

Here it is again: "Good lyrics are simply lyrics that do what they are intended to do"
-Frank Zappa

Let me boldly suggest a new version:

"A lyric is good when it does a good job. What that job is can be an intentional job or an unintentional one, or both"

Gah.. You see the difficulty of defining quality here, yes?

Lyrics can do so much. They can tell a story with a beginning and a middle and an end. Or they can be abstract and dreamy. The can put images in your head, take you places. They can be sexy, make your cheeks and ears red. They can make critical and/or angry reports of social injustices. They can be funny and make you laugh uncontrollably, and so on and so forth.

You do NOT at all always have to understand the lyrics of a song.

It doesn't really matter if it is a tune on the radio (or whatever more modern media) or it's the tune you are writing or have written. You don't have to understand it. It also nice if you do. But it is not a must.

Allowing for the receiver of any art expression to misunderstand is an important part of the beauty of it all.

I even dare to say: isn't ALL interpretation in its essence more about misunderstanding than understanding? Or at least equally so?

When you understand or misunderstand, i.e. interpret, you become an interactive part of the piece of art that is the song.

The self-given flip side of that coin is: When you give you your listener or your audience permission to understand or misunderstand, i.e. interpret, you let them become an interactive part of the piece of art that is the song. This is the most powerful shit possible. In essence, if a lyric makes you feel anything, it is doing its job and that will always be a good thing, in its own way. Beyond that the rest are, in comparison, pure technicalities.

For example the feeling of flow in the diction. Or the sense of direction and having a "red thread" in the storytelling. Or how smart or witty the rhymes are. Sometimes a good lyric is just... to the point. Take for instance a James Brown song. You can pick almost any of them. Let's choose "Get Up Offa That Thing" If you just read the words by themselves, they aren't much, are they? But together with the music?

Pure gold.

So do they do the "job"? Absolutely. On more than one level. They are short and concise yet abstract and insinuating. They are effective and percussive and don't get in the way of the groove. Are they as great when read as standalone lyrics taken out of their context? No, not really, but they were never intended to be taken out of context. So, the context is of great importance to the quality of a lyric.

Ralph Murphy, for many years a top ASCAP guy (passed away in 2019), often gave lectures on the art of songwriting, where he drove the point that, most of the time, it is a good thing to choose what element of the song you are writing that is to take precedence. Which element is to carry the most information. Then after deciding that, the other elements take a step back in support of that up-front element.

These elements are:

Lyrics
Rhythm (Groove)
Harmony
Melody
Arrangement

Let's say that we are writing a song with a lot of words and information in the lyrics. If we make other the elements info-loaded, for instance harmony-wise, with a lot of fancy, intricate chords and then with a really advanced melody on top of a busy groove in an ambitious arrangement, these other elements *might* divert attention and take away from the power of the lyrics. They might shade it or steal its thunder.

Examples of when the lyrics are given the most important role, and the other elements are made simpler are plentiful. All Bob Dylan songs for instance. Or even all Singer/Songwriter songs. Perhaps also most country songs. (At least old school country before production became such a big deal).

In Funk music every other element takes a step back to let the groove take the spotlight. The horn arrangements can be stellar and allowed some space though.

In Jazz music the lyrics often take a step back, in the sense that they are many times easy to follow and to the point. Not so abstract. Simplistic yet clever, perhaps one could say... Or naive... if one is in that mood. (Not ALWAYS, mind you... just often).

Jazz instead puts its money on a harmony that can get extremely intricate, and of course rhythm.

Few artists have pulled of the great feat of top-loading all of these elements and still produce great songs. Joni Mitchell, David Bowie, Queen, Frank Zappa, Billy Joel, Paul Simon. Some Beatles-stuff, Steely Dan... There are of course plenty more names to add to this list, but you probably get the idea. It is a difficult feat to try and fill every element of a song with enough information to carry its own artistic weight. A really tall order. And if you want to give it a go you definitely should.

The point of telling you about this conundrum – that it's often a good idea to let one element take precedence – is to give you a tool of thinking: Should I keep the other elements more basic in order to put emphasis on this one element?

So when I now will try and write a song "lyrics first", I will also decide to put the lyrics up front, making the other elements simpler.

Here we go....

STARTING A NEW SONG FROM LYRICS

As I now go on a treasure hunt for a lyrical idea that inspires me, I turn to my trusted little book of one-liners. After a bit of sweating and suffering, and allowing myself to suck and sound silly, I get this:

We're living in Crazy Town
Crazy Town
We're living in Crazy Town
But I'm beginning to know my way around

It is not much at this point, but it feels nice somehow. "Crazy Town" can be any situation that you find yourself in, that is bad and feels hard to remedy and change. All you can do is adapt. It can be a local situation in your life or the world as a whole or anything in between. But this is the open end of the funnel I have described earlier. Meaning that I now can tell just about any story about any bad situation. Let's try.

I can remember what I first saw
The secret behind your smile
A story kept safe behind the thickest walls
No one was let inside

My heart then was set on a mission
To make that drawbridge fall
To win your trust and admission
But now I know we're all

Living in Crazy Town Crazy Town
We're living in Crazy Town
But I'm starting to know my way around

I'm thinking that the second verse should be kept down to four lines instead of eight. I will try to get a Middle eight with lyrics in this one, so I need to keep it as tight as possible. Second verses need to develop what has been said before, so what is the story so far?

The "Self" or "I" or first person perspective in the lyrics, takes fancy to someone. This person is very private and has a strong or even problematically high sense of integrity. He struggles to get into her life. But once he gets in there, he discovers it is not as pleasant a place to be as he had hoped it would be. It is instead, "Crazy Town". In verse two we should probably learn more about what really is so crazy about this town...

Woke up one morning stuck under your thumb
Mostly the fault was mine
Don't think even Dunning-Kruger met someone as dumb
But right here I draw the line

This is Crazy Town
Crazy Town
We're living in Crazy Town
Where we're starting to know our way
Around this town

That´s Crazy Town
Crazy Town
But enough is enough and today I'm homeward bound.
No more Crazy Town
No more Crazy Town
No more Crazy Town

There we have it. At least a rough draft, since I haven't tried to sing it yet. We never learned that much more about the specifics of the craziness. But being vague can also serve a purpose. My first attempt to sing the chorus led me to a kind of Bluegrassy feeling. Here it is after a few run-throughs:

Crazy Town

I can remember what I first saw
The secret behind your smile
A story kept safe behind the thickest walls
No one was let inside

My heart then was set on a mission
To make that drawbridge fall
To win your trust and admission
But now I know we're all

Living in Crazy Town
Crazy Town
We're living in Crazy Town
But I'm starting to know my way around

Woke up one morning stuck under your thumb
Mostly the fault was mine
Don't think even Dunning-Kruger met someone as dumb
But right here I draw the line

Living in Crazy Town
Crazy Town
We're living in Crazy Town
Where we're starting to know our way
Around this town
That's Crazy Town
Crazy Town
But enough is enough and today I'm homeward bound

No more Crazy Town
No more Crazy Town
No more Crazy Town

Now we have the lyrics, then all we need is music! I found this simple but nice Crosby-Stills-Nash and Young type of chord riff on my iPhone memo that I could sing the chorus over. That riff was then followed by a Bluegrassy fast riff. I felt a pull towards Bluegrass early on for this idea so I kept that idea around for a while. But when I started to record a demo of the song, I first played a rhythm guitar to a classic train beat. Then next I began to play some bass over the guitar. I made up a pretty nice little bass theme over the CSNY type riff that will be both intro and later the chorus. Let's call that the B part, since it is also the chorus.

But when the next part, that fast Bluegrassy part came, the only way I could make the bass fit under that was the classic Bluegrass 1-5 bass. Nothing wrong with that. Absolutely not. But coming after the CSNY style B part with the nice bass theme, it felt... dull...
So, I continued with the same bass groove but with the chord sequence from the Bluegrass part. This also lent itself to a bit more syncopated feel to that riff.

This in turn rendered the Bluegrass riffing useless on top of that syncopated groove. But this felt much was more like a natural development of the CSNY part.

So, on top of this new feel, I need a new theme-riff-thing...

Almost immediately a new one popped up in my head. A guitar melody thingy. So, now it's more like something of a... I don't know... CNSY/Bruce Hornsby feeling? If that group existed, they would have a really long name. Crosby-Stills-Nash-Young- Hornsby.

But I really dig the way a tune can take unexpected turns like this. Perhaps especially when starting "lyrics first".

A little time jump: This week I have recorded drums for the songs written in this book (so these lines are added in after), I the beautiful studio Spinroad (www.spinroadstudios.com). And when I sent the demo of this song to the drummer, I intentionally did not include any programmed drums, in order to not restrict his imagination of what the drums might play on the track. Sometimes this way you can get wonderful new spins on your songs. He heard the vers as a half tempo feel as opposed to the uptempo feel of the rest of the tune. I really dug that idea and we kept it.

So the arrangement has turned out as follows:

B (As intro)
i (Second part intro)
A (Verse)
B (Chorus)

i (half, as an intermission)

A
B
A (Solo)
B (Solo) B
B
i (as outro)

Ending with breaks.
This time when we came around to the sticky point after

the second chorus, that is when we had first Introduced and then Established, as we remember from The Bernstein Principle, it is high time to introduce a Change. I went with an improvised solo on first the verse and then kept the solo going into the chorus. Then the vocals come back for a double chorus. But, and this part I am quite pleased with:

The CSNY style A part is really only a Bm and a C chord on top of a static D in the bass, and by now we are getting pretty bored with that. So for the double chorus in the end I leave the static D bass and harmonize these chords instead with spelled out bass notes. And to my ears it resulted in beautiful harmonic both lift and needed release.

Crazy Town

Martin Carlberg

2
Mostly the fault was mine Don´t think even Dunning Kruger met someone as dumb But
right here I draw the line Living in Crazy Town Crazy
Town Living in Crazy Town But I´m beginning to know my way around
This is Crazy Town Crazy Town
Lining in Crazy Town Where we´re starting to know our way around this town
That´s Crazy Town Living in Crazy Town But enough´s enough
and
today I´m homeward bound No more Crazy Town No more Crazy

CHORDS AND HARMONY

> "Harmony is the ocean that melody sets sail on"
>
> — *Unknown*

It is bound to get a bit technical now. And a bit divisive. Writers and musicians that are super intuitive often detest, or at least shy away from, this type of knowledge and information about the technical side of music and harmony. Others have ventured light years further into this realm of musical structure than I ever have or ever will.

For the first category, the theory haters, every word in this chapter might be as understandable as ancient Greek. For the second category, the theory lovers, the information will all probably be just above entry level stuff.

So, this chapter might be for those readers, who like me, are caught somewhere in between these two categories. Somewhere in the middle. With a little of both love and hate for this theoretical side of art. I guess that I do have a pretty good basic understanding, but I find that the more you learn, the more you realize how much more there is to know. And how much you don't know.
Still, I know enough to get by.

And since I only know enough to get by, and since this is such a towering giant of a topic, how could I possibly dream to fit anything even remotely comprehensive in these few pages, that isn't just an embarrassing pale shadow of a shrapnel of what this topic is, or can be?? The only way to go, at least for me who is the one writing this book, is to simplify.

I will just tell you about the things I use and how I look at music theory. If nothing else, you will by my limited view of this topic, learn something about the level of knowledge one can get away with.

Or something like that.

Also, there is no way of knowing what level you are at in this area. Should I aim high with delicate harmonic tricks, or low with only the basics?

With that said...

What is Harmony?

Well, to start at the absolute beginning, certain frequencies resonate together and create harmony when played simultaneously.
In western music (as in western countries, and NOT the middle east), we have divided one octave of sound waves into 12 equally spaced pitches of the given a value we have chosen to call 100 cents. 100 cents makes up what is called a semitone. That's one fret on a guitar. 200 cents

is called a whole step. Seven of these twelve, we have decided, sound the best together and we have make them the diatonic major scale.

If we then also name these notes of the diatonic scale, we make them and their musical function easier to talk about:

A B C D E F G

In between those notes we have

A# or Bb
C# or Db
D# or Eb
F# or Gb
G# or Ab

But then we come to the function of these notes in a musical context and naming those functions. The first note of the major scale, any major scale that is, is called the "One" or the "Tonic" or the "Root"

The second note of the major scale is most often simply referred as the "Second". The classical name "supertonic" exists, but I never ever hear it in practice.

The third note of the scale is perhaps arguably the most important one, when played alongside the root. Or one could say that it is the interval that carries the most power for changing how you perceive an interval or chord, since it is the interval between the root and the third that makes a chord major or minor. Or if you will, feel happy or sad. If the third is minor it is three semitones from the root and if it is a major third it is four semitones from the root. The third note of a major scale is most often referred to as the "Third" or "Major Third" Major third is to distinguish it from the "Minor Third" that is three semitones from the root instead of four. The Archaic name "The Mediant" also exists for this interval but also I never hear it used.

The Fourth note of the major scale is both interesting and not interesting. One of the reasons it might be viewed as interesting is, that it is regarded to be not interesting.
(Forgive me for being silly and messing with you when the topic is this strict.)

What I mean is this: Many Jazz artists avoid the fourth as the plague. They see it as an empty, vulgar "avoid note". I don't agree, and I don't really see why they perceive the fourth this way.

On the other hand, I do hear and recognize the special sound that it makes when jazz players stay away from it. It is a bit of a "nothing note" perhaps? A bit bland. This might be because of its kinship with the Fifth, since it is a Fifth inverted? And the fifth (we are getting slightly ahead of ourselves here) is the "cleanest" interval.

An example we seem to be coming back to for all sorts of different reasons is Deep Purple's "Smoke On The Water".
In the riff we find a classic case of a people thinking

mistakenly that it is a Fourth, when it is in fact actually (in its function) a Fifth.

The way that is played is of course in fourths, playing the D and G string together. But since the key is G minor, the note D assumes the role of the fifth when played with the G. A fifth, only an octave down and a fourth below the root. Since the chord implied is a G chord.

The Fourth is also called the "Subdominant", and as a chord, more than a single note, the subdominant function is a very, very important one, so this is good to remember.

Tip, or hack, or whatever:
A very common chord progression in pop/rock is IV-V-I
In Jazz the equivalent is II-V-I
Try switching the root of the IV chord to II root or vice versa at any time and see what it does to the sound and feel of your song. (This in essence makes the IV a II or vice versa.)

The Fifth is the faithful companion of the root. It is an interval that, along with the root, has the most aligned overtones. These overtones and their alignment or misalignment can easily be heard whenever playing a fifth on a string instrument with strings that can be bent. Play the root and the fifth as a "rock guitar chord" and bend the fifth ever so slightly. That out-of-tune-flutter is the overtones going out of alignment. This is also why, when playing distorted sounds, most often of course on electric guitar, this "chord" of Root-Fifth is the one most commonly used since it makes for a strong and "pure" sound without any dissonance or fluttering of misaligned overtones. This is because, when a sound is distorted, overtones become more pronounced.

The Fifth is very useful as a "Pedal tone", meaning that it can be kept around even if the chords change diatonically, or you can bounce off of it with any other note of the diatonic scale and against any diatonic chord

The Fifth is also called the "Dominant", which is a term used frequently and should be both remembered and understood. Well... understood or understood. I don't know that I fully do understand myself.

I view the Dominant as the main "counter weight" to the Root. If the Root or Tonic is the "Home" chord, then the Dominant chord is the maximum "Away" chord but in a "Away-but-wants-to-go-home" way. The Dominant has a feel of direction to it. It wants to go "Home". The Dominant wants to lead to the Root. And since it is the maximum of "Away", we have a bit of a "What happens in Vegas, stays in Vegas" situation. Now: "What happens in the Dominant, stays in the Dominant". What I mean is that "Anything goes" or just about anything at least, if done with enough conviction.
This means that the Dominant can be extended with just about any and all notes if the circumstances call for it.

Try these on for size in the key of A-major (E is the dominant in the key of A-Major):

E7(E,G#,B,D)
E9 (E,G#,B,D,F#)
E11(E.G#,B,D,F#.A)
E13(E,G#,B,D,F#,A,C#)
E+(E,G#,C)
E7b9(E,G#,B,D,F)

With the right conviction, any of the 12 chromatic notes can be played over these chords. The great Pat Metheny once said that the only note he wouldn't or couldn't use over a dominant chord, was the major 7th, or as he put it, that was the only note he "couldn't hear" over a dominant chord. In spite of this I strongly remember Django Reinhardt playing a major 7th over a dominant chord and thereby proving Metheny "wrong" by making it work beautifully. Dissonant but still beautiful. You have to have a really big pair of balls to pull that off though.

It is a huge understatement to say, both the Blues sound and a large portion of the jazz sound are built around the heavy use of the dominant sound. Also making use of it not only in the classic dominant position or for the classic dominant function. It uses it for this as well of course but also for the tension it creates in its own right.

Most Blues tunes for instance, are based around three dominant chords. The first is used as the Root chord. Let's use the key of A as an example.

So we have an A7 as the Root or Tonic chord.
The second chord is used in the Fourth or Subdominant position, D7 The third chord is a Fifth up from the root making it a E7

This gives us a whole new ballgame of note choices, and we only have the possibility of scratching that surface here. Also, this is supposed to be a book about songwriting and not about note choices for Jazz or Blues improvisation.

So I'll settle for this simple scratching of the surface:

On the Tonic chord (A7 in this case), you can use both the minor or major pentatonic for melody. The noteworthy (pun!) thing is that both the major and minor thirds work. Two distinctively different sounds and feel, but both work a charm.

You can even take this idea one step further and play or sing the minor third and the minor pentatonic scale against a major chord that has no dominant 7, one that is a perfectly normal major chord, and thereby imply a dominant bluesy feel.

Example:
Ain't That Good News – Sam Cooke
Did you listen to Sam? Gutsy innit?

One step even further is to use the minor pentatonic over fully major and not dominant chord changes. Now this for sure requires a hefty set of balls to make work.

Example:
Mick Jagger's harmonica solo on The Roling Stones cover rendition of Bob Dylan's Like A Rolling Stone.

Another example is just about any John Mayer guitar solo over a major chord progression, where he often use both major and minor pentatonic. Major to be "nice" and minor for attitude.

You can often lean more heavily on the minor third on the subdominant chord of a major key, since the minor third of the key will be the dominant 7 of the subdominant chord, giving it a dominant bluesy sound.

So if you can use both the major and the minor third over a dominant chord, and if you can manage to imply and convey the dominant feel even on a straight major chord; is then, one might ask oneself, the opposite also true?
Can you use the major third over a minor chord?

My slightly generalizing answer would have to be no. This is REALLY difficult to make work. But having said that... I have again heard perhaps the GOAT of melodic players; Django Reinhardt pull this feat off as well. So...

In essence, there are what Miles Davis would call the "Butter notes" meaning the notes that comfortably fit over a chord. Then there are notes that are "off". Some players can make any of these notes work at any time. It is difficult to decode in detail why. But to play with confidence is definitely one of the top ingredients in the recipe of how to make odd notes sound "right". Attitude and context, perhaps.

The Sixth is the classic interval added to the end chords of pop and rock tunes from the late 50-ties and 60-ties.

Example: "Help" and "She Loves You" – The Beatles

I am not sophisticated enough to elaborate that much on the sixth, other than a few small thoughts. This is where the relative minor chord in a key (we will get to that) is found.

It is a nice colouring note quite often. Try it on for instance on both the Root, subdominant and the Dominant chord as an add6, this means 1,3,5,6 and no 7th

A chord like that is most often just written and notated as E6 or Bb6 or C6 (or whatever). The "no seventh" is for some reason taken as a given.

On a major chord I think the sixth makes the chord "softer"

On a minor chord the major sixth will create the typical Gypsy Jazz French feel.

Example: "Minor Swing" – Django Reinhardt

To be fair, the added sixth for colour is all over the Gypsy

Jazz style, on both major and minor chords.

Also try adding it for an extra expensive shimmery sound when you do the "minor subdominant thing"

What is the minor subdominant thing?

It is when you lower the third of the subdominant chord from its normal major to a minor. It is not actually called the "minor subdominant thing", but that is kind of what it is.

Example: "In My Life" – The Beatles

To simplify: If we for instance are in the key of G Major, go from G to C and then to C minor. Then try from G and go straight to C minor. Then try adding the 6th to the C minor (the note A) also try adding the 9th (the note A) Making it a Cm69
Pretty, yes?

Whenever I need to instantly recall the sound of the sixth, for whatever reason. I use a little trick. I think of the "Ray Charles lick". Now Ray Charles of course had many licks, but this was one of his go-to-licks. It goes 6-5 glissando down to 2 then 1.

But I just start the lick and stay on the first note

Ray does the lick all the time but here is one example: 2.20 into "Hallelujah (I Love Her So)" he sings "Don't you know" . And on the word "Don't" the note is the 6th

I suggest you make your own tricks like this to instantly recall the sound of every interval.

Another example for finding the Sixth is the tune "Stand By Me" by Ben E King. I bet you can recall the sound of the opening phrase:

When the night...has come

The note on the word "night", that note is the sixth.

"Gravity" by John Mayer is another great example, where the vocal melody starts on the sixth.

Come to think of it, let's throw in a little short list of song examples where the melody starts with a certain interval.

Half note or Minor Second

"Jaws"- John Williams
"Isn't She Lovely" - Stevie Wonder
"As Times Goes by" - Herman Hupfeld
Second

"Happy Birthday"

Minor Third

"I've Put A Spell On You"

Major Third

"When The Saints Go Marching In" – Traditional

Forth

I actually found it pretty hard to find a melody that starts with a fourth.

All the examples I found are in function a reversed fifth. And since everyone else writing on this topic seems to be contented with using these examples, so will I (grudgingly).

What I mean is, that a ton of melodies start off with a pick up from a fourth below the tonic. And the fourth below the tonic is the fifth an octave down. Therefore, the function of the notes are really 5-1 and not 4-1. But this is perhaps semantics, and you will see this functional fifth described as a fourth everywhere else, so you are probably better off disregarding my take on that completely, and view "Smoke On The Water" and these following pick-up lines as examples of fourths.

Examples of this are:

"Love Me Tender" (Vera Mattson, Elvis Presley)
"Amazing Grace" (John Newton)

"We Wish You A Merry Christmas" – Traditional

Minor(or flat) fifth/ Tritone

"Maria From West Side Story" (Bernstein/Sondheim)

I tend to cheat a bit with this one and use the chanting vocal line from Led Zeppelins "Immigrant Song". It goes from tonic to the at fifth, but via the fifth. So 1- 5-5b

Fifth

"Twinkle Twinkle Little Star" (Traditional)

"Top Gun Anthem" (Harold Feltermeyer" Hugo Peretti, Luigi Creatore, George David Weiss)

"Can't Help Falling In Love" (Hugo Peretti, Luigi Creatore, George David Weiss)

Minor sixth

Couldn't think of one. But the Usher song "Yeah" uses it in the synth melody it goes 1-5 then 1-6 the 6 being the minor sixth. Same thing-ish in Ozzys "Crazy Train" and "Lose Yourself" by Eminem.

Major sixth

"My Bonnie Lies Over The Ocean" (Traditional)

Dominant Seven

"The Winner Takes It All" (Andersson/Ulvaeus)

Major Seven

"Take On Me" (Magne Furuholmen, Morten Harket och Pål Waaktaar-Savoy)

Octave

" Somewhere Over The Rainbow" (Harold Arlen)

Moving on...

The Major seventh is quite interesting in many ways. The first thing that comes to my mind, is that although the natural 7th of the major scale is one semitone below the octave root, the NAME "the seventh" is instead used to describe the Dominant Seventh which is another half step down. So when people are being sloppy in their musical lingo and just say "the seventh", chances are that they mean the dominant seventh and not the major seventh. Just a good thing to know and remember.

The sound of the major seventh by itself (meaning root-major 7 played together or consecutively) leaves me with a feeling of something being "unfinished" or perhaps is on its way towards conclusion.

A full Major 7th chord (1-3-5-major7) has a rich, soft and "friendly" sound to my ears. "Kind" even. "Expensive" perhaps. Lends an air of sophistication.
It can even be viewed upon and used as an effect.

Listen to the lovely use of it in the song "To Be Young (Is To Be Sad
Is To Be High) by Ryan Adams off of his 2001 debut album "Heartbreaker". The tune is a bluesy, rockabilly style tune when -lo-and-behold – all of a sudden, the tonic goes from a dominant seven feel to a major seventh feel. And it is like the whole world opens up. I find myself transported to a magic place.

So...

To create a basic chord we play three notes simultaneously (at once), namely every other note of the major scale. We can then extend the chords, or as it is often called "colour" them, by adding more notes in the every-other-note fashion. Adding the 7-9-11-13
The 9th is the same note as the 2 note, but one octave up. Actually, it can be more than one octave up and it will still be called the 9th.

Same goes for the 11th that's the same note as the 4th and the 13th is same as 6th at least one octave up.

These extensions are "diatonic" which means, in practice, that they're in the key of the piece or section. If you add extensions outside of that, like b9, #9 and so on, they are "alternative" or "outside" extensions often resulting in a dissonance with harmonic tension.

The reason for the idea of using numbers higher than 8, even though 9 is the same actual note as 2 and so on, is because if a tight and close harmonic interval as a 1 and 2 as in tonic and second, is played in a closed position as in for instance the white keys next to each other C and D. And then the continued C major chord on top of that, the E and the G. The D stuck in between the C and the E will cause quite a hefty mesh of harmonic soup.

Maybe that is what you want, and if that is the case, all is good.

Often it is not. Then all you have to do is move that D note up an octave, and voila... The blend is rich and open, every note clear and sitting well in the mix of the chord.

And using the numbers 9, 11 and 13 indicates, from the start, that these added notes are meant to be separated from the root of your chord by at least one octave.

In between every chord there is a non-diatonic transition chord.

Or several such solutions. These are useful songwriting tools.

Although more examples can be made, I will present two

(or three) (or four) similar options.

1. Major chord with the third in the bass
2. Diatonic 7 chord with the third in the bass
3. Minor 7b5 (sometimes called half-diminished)
4. Diminished (Minor thirds stacked)

Example 1: Major chord with the third in the bass

C A/C# Dm B/Eb Em F D/F# G E/G# Am F#/Bb

In this example these following chords are diatonic, meaning "in key”. The key is in this case C-major:

C Dm Em F G Am Bm7b5

These following chords are in this case non-diatonic, ”passing chords”:

A/C# B/Eb D/F# E/G# F#/Bb

The passing chords can be exchanged to fit your taste with the others I listed here:

A/C# for **A7/C#** or **C#m7-5** or **C#dim**

B/Eb for **B7/Eb** or **Ebm7-5** or **Ebdim**

D/F# for **D7/F#** or **Dm7-5** or **Ddim**

E/G# for **E7/G#** or **G#m7-5** or **G#dim**

F#/Bb for **F#7/Bb** or **F#7-5** or **F#dim**

Each solution or choice of passing chord has its own flavour, feel and sound. To me, I have put them in order of perceived complexity. The major chord with the third in the bass, is the "nicest" sounding. Easiest on the ear. The most "pop" sounding passing chord.

But such nicety is not always what you want. So the other options are often to me, increasingly richer harmonic choices. And I try them on to see which one best fits the mood of the moment in the song I am working on.
There are probably more alternatives to substitute that I can't think of at the moment and even more options that I don't know about. But these are what I normally use.

Another nice tool is to have some options to what can be done to spice up each diatonic chord.

The Tonic chord

On the tonic chord, a classic move is to make it a dominant 7 before going to the subdominant.
Often it is used to signal that change.

Example: C C7 F

My idea of why this, and things like this, work so well, are due to harmonic or melodic "lines". In this case, if we continue the example of Major as tonic...

In the sound of the Major, in its subtext, in its fabric, is the subconscious sound of the major 7. By making it a dominant 7, that means that that note is on the move. B to Bb. So, what is the next position for that note? It is an A note, which is the third of the F major chord.

To make another example how "lines" give context to chords, or how chords can make a unmelodic line melodic is this classic:

Let's make a chromatic line.

The single notes **C B Bb A Ab G**

Just a simple chromatic line. Nothing melodic about it. It just is what it is. But put it in this context:

Cmajor Cmajor7 C7 Fmajor Fminor Cmajor

All of a sudden, every note has purpose. Fits. Has direction. The bland chromatic line becomes a melodic (albeit rudimentary) line.

But is it the chords that make melody of the notes or the notes that give purpose to the chords?

Well, I say it goes both ways, that they, in essence, are the same.

Let's say we have a minor tonic. Although seldom used in Pop and Rock, the minor tonic can be turned into major for effect. Often a transitional effect. Often again it is before going to a minor Subdominant.

Example: Am A Dm

Or like this: **Am A/C# Dm**

A governing factor (or rather THE governing factor) is what the melody is doing. If the melody is the note C, then the option of turning the minor tonic of Am into Amajor is in this case a bad idea, since C is the minor third of Am and therefore suggesting this chord. If the melody goes to ANY other note than C over the Am, then it can be done.

Example: Django Reinhardt and Stephane Grappelli's version of "It Don't Mean A Thing"

A fine print delicacy of this version, that even professional people I have played the song with seem to have missed, is that although the tune is in the key of Gm, the little delicacy here is that when the melody land on the last note of the first line, which is the root note G, the chord is not the expected Gm but they instead play a G Major. (Or a G6 to be precise but that the chord is major is the point.)

It works simply because the melody at that instance, as I said, is playing the root note G.

That leaves the third of the chord, the note that makes a chord minor or major, open for interpretation.
We have now written three songs so far, in ”real time” here. The first one ”Go Out On Your Own” was written from the starting point of needing/wanting to write a song, but starting from scratch without any previous idea for the piece whatsoever.

The second one, ”Land On My Feet”, from the starting point of needing/wanting to write a song for yourself, but from an existing idea. In this case a riff.

The third one, ”Crazy Town”, actually also from the starting point of needing/wanting to write a song for yourself, but from an existing idea. But in this case a lyric first.

We are still to write a song from this perspective:

Needing/wanting to write a commissioned song to a brief that contains directional information.

So, let's do that.

But before we do that, let's first talk some more on the topic that is in the actual title of this book!

WRITING ON DEMAND

I remember clearly and vividly the occasion when I was really first asked to write anything with a deadline and with specific demands. Admittedly, I had already been writing on a kind of more general demand for a while, but since the production music company I was writing for was quite new back then, I was allowed for the first whole year or so, to write and submit whatever I wanted. The music would then be judged on its own merit and quality, and if they liked it they bought it.

The only rejection I really had was two pieces that I submitted right at the beginning, and because of that rejection, I quickly made the effort to decode what it was that they seemed to like (and dislike), and therefore, ultimately, would want to buy from me. (I had when I left the company a 99,93% approval rate and had "sold" 531 pieces.)
This "general" writing on demand is really quite uncommon nowadays, and is not what I refer to by the title of this chapter. The chapter could well have been called "Writing on Specific Demand", but for some reason that just didn´t have the same ring to it.

But in one stroke, or rather with one single phone call, that whole situation of just being able to write whatever I wanted and getting paid for it, came to an end, or at least changed forever.

Like I said, the phone rang.
It was the guy from the production music company. The brief (the request) they had for me was a commission for five Latin dance instrumental pieces.

This meant that I needed to not only write these pieces, but also record them, mix them and then submit finished masters to be scrutinized by business professionals.

All this needed to be finished within two weeks. I remember hearing myself saying "Yes of course, no problem". Then we hung up and the conversation was over.

I had now, apparently, agreed to deliver five original pieces of Latin music, fully produced in two weeks!! Did I know anything about Latin music? No. Not really.

I was, as you might imagine, in a bit of a fix!

But almost in parallel with the rising panic and terror over the humiliation that would obviously ensue upon my upcoming failure to deliver anything but crap, and the following dishonourable discharge from the production company, a simple but transforming feeling of "come on now, let's do this" was forming in the back of my mind. Within the hour this growing feeling had far surpassed the negative ones, and off I went in search of a way to get this both inspiring and scary job done.

I for some reason, just by chance (not that it mattered) started with a Tango, and began an archaeological investigation into what Tango is. How is it defined? What are the typical aesthetics involved?

Disclaimer: I have no idea if what follows is in any way a remotely accurate description of Tango. It is not even meant to be. It doesn't even actually need to be. It will only serve as an example of my process of subjective analysis and breaking down this (or any) style or type of music. So, this is only a description of how I at this point in time perceived Tango.

What I found was this:

Tango is a couple's dance developed in Buenos Aires 'and Montevideo's immigrant quarters in the late 1800s.

Since it is a dance, it needs to stay within the limits of a certain Beats Per Minute (BPM) range. Some text I found set this BPM range to be between 118-130.

But after listening to the tempo of a number of songs I found tempos as low as 110 and as high as 140 BPM.

However, the most common tempo seemed to land most songs I surveyed at around 120 BPM

It has a kind of marching beat feel to it, with equal weight on every quarter note. But it seems to me that there is an added eight note, that is kind of a common feature,

between the 4th beat and the 1st beat of every next measure.
Like so: 1...2...3...4 and 1...2...3...4 and...
I do not know if this is a tango requirement, but it is often there.

(I also read that Tango classically is viewed to be counted in 2/4, but I do not hear or feel it that way and will therefore ignore that.)

Tango often has an A-part in a Minor key and a B-part in a Major key, but over the same tonic.
For example: If the A-part is in C Minor then the B-part is in C Major
Or vice versa: The A-part can be Major and the B-part Minor

The bass commonly plays a line that goes something like this:

Tango bass 1a

Traditional

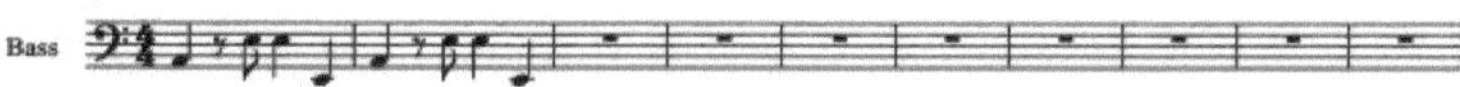

The chords used strike me as basic 1-3-5 chords (meaning tonic, third and fifth) and seldom use upper extensions. Well, upper extensions are used, but – dare I say – sparingly, and mostly in string arrangements and such,

when they occur.
And that's about all I dug up on the subject.

(Note: I have later learned that Tango on the contrary indeed often use richly colourful upper chord extensions, but at the time this was my limited view, and no one it seems, died from it)

So let's try and see if we can draw from this new found knowledge, and use this info like building blocks, Lego pieces if you will, to attempt to write ourselves a Tango tune right now.

The way I like to do it, if I am working in the studio, is to get a beat going. So, I will make a little simple tango marching beat, for now at 120 bpm.

This is to keep the ideas that will (hopefully) present themselves in the right rhythmical ballpark.

After some initial fiddling around, I decide on C-Minor and to base the melody on a little theme chromatically circling around the 5th.

My basic idea for the A-part then, is this:

The last chord of the A-part is the V chord, the dominant chord. This is both typical for the style and optimal because sonically it can point back to a tonic in both Minor or Major.

Since the A-part was in C Minor, I now want the B-part in C Major.
And because the last chord of the A-part is the V chord, I don't need to do anything else to make this key change work. I can simply and seamlessly start the B-Part in C Major.

Again, after fiddling around a bit to find a compatible theme that feels like a natural extension and progression from the A-part in Minor, I come up with this:

Now, more than one thing can be done here to turn this into a "complete" piece of music. There are plenty of options and possible roads to take.

The choice of what to do next can depend on a few different factors.

Firstly, if this is actually an order for a production music piece, like my original brief was, then the piece should be about 2.00 min in length. If this is what the tune is, for it is in fact important not to overwork it. The reason for that is simply, that if you do, you might accidentally raise the bar of what level of work is required and also expected from you in the future, but for the same amount of money.

So, in this case I would come up with an effective, in-style intro, then go ABAB and then finally wrap it up with a suitable ending.
Often an ascending arpeggio and a short hit.

It is important to remember that with production music, cliché is your friend. The feeling of the music when added to a visual video feature should be immediate and obvious. For this purpose – production music purpose that is –there is no point in trying to re-invent the wheel. It is even counterproductive. So if the brief is for a Tango, then what you deliver must be a clear cut, obvious Tango.
Or at least (and this might be the big secret to it all) it must sound like a Tango.

If I on the other hand, were to write this Tango for myself, and for my own repertoire, I might indeed still arrange it as simply described above. But only if it feels optimal for the piece of music. I would, in this case, spend some more effort and time trying to sense if anything could be added to the above arrangement to improve upon it. Perhaps a C-part? And if a C-part is added, should it be style typical or should it be an "all bets are off", anything-goes, kind of C-part?

Let's try and come up with a C-part and see how it goes...

I fiddled around a bit and went with a solution I tend to favour.
The C-part that takes you to places the other parts of the piece don't go to.

I am gonna use... Queen style chords and play Albert King licks on top. Because I want to.

Again: if this was on a commissioned production on

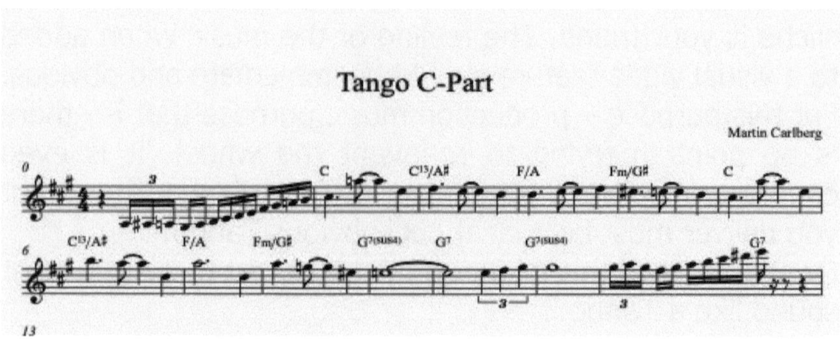

demand, all of that stuff that is not typical for the style would be out the window.

How do you like this?:

A bit off centre, I know, but fresh to the ear and a wee bit fun and interesting, yes? I think so!

And when you come back to the B-part, it feels and warm and welcome, yes? I dig it!

When time came to record this tango, I got the idea to make it a vocal tune. As previously stated, when you deliver this as a production piece, keep it simple! ABABB then finito!

But now I am releasing this music alongside of the book, and because of that, I feel like having some fun with it.

So now we need some lyrics. I feel that they should be "in

style". There will be enough of the opposite going on anyway. What to sing about in a Tango? Feelings. Love. These subjects are a given. But something has to justify the story being set in a tango.
Easy solution: Let's place it there geographically.
I immediately google Argentina (google is your friend), and find a website telling me that spring is an especially lovely time of the year in this part of the world. Let us use that.

I had heard Buenos Aires was pretty in spring
Purple Jacaranda blossoms and the hummingbirds sing

I found that stuff about the Jacaranda blossoms and the hummingbirds on some travel website too. Tom Waits call that "furniture", when you don't just say for instance blossoms and birds, but what blossoms and what birds. You are putting furniture in your room. Making the picture more alive. Like Van Morrison in Tupelo Honey. He doesn't just sing "You're as sweet as Honey". No, instead he googles (maybe he didn't google it since the song was released in 1971) but he researches what is the best honey and found it to be Tupelo Honey. So now his lyrics had more furniture, was more specific. It goes:

> "You're as sweet, as Tupelo Honey"
>
> — *Van Morrison*

We now have set the stage and need to introduce both our male female leading characters.

What do you think about this:

I had heard Buenos Aires was pretty in spring
Purple Jacaranda blossoms and the hummingbirds sing
But nothing could have prepared me
For something as beautiful as your hazel eyes

A bit cheesy, I know.... But, in my defence... The whole notion of singing to this track leads me to feel that this is done for fun. For the hell of it. We are playing with clichés here. Therefor we can get away with being a bit cheesy, and still sleep at night with a clear conscious. We can go all in and be "pekoral". You remember the Swedish word meaning "overly emotional"? Having said that, what would be a good thing for the chorus, along those lines? A Shakespeare quote! Yes!

This approach does not in any way disrespect the wonderful and vibrant genre and history of Tango but is simply a way of staying true to the way the song has come about. It started as play with what I found the clichés of the genre to be. Which for the purpose of writing music on demand (or any type of creative process), is a very good practice. Therefor it needed a continuation of that thought. I found this Shakespeare quote:

Be Still My Beating Heart
Be still and play your part
If I am to win her hand tonight
We must be in this together
Right from the start

This language is archaic, for sure, but I am having fun. I also reference the Swedish GENIUS songwriter Evert Taube, who wrote a lot about Argentina in a language that was current then but is regarded archaic now. Having listened a lot to him, this is a bit of an homage, I guess. Or perhaps it will have him rotating in his grave...

Note: I later learned that Sting already had a song called "Be Still My Beating Heart" on his 1987 album "...Nothing Like The Sun"
But since A) Titles are not subject to copyright B) Sting also nipped it from Shakespeare. So it absolutely stays. Now back to the narrative...

Also, if you noticed, in this case I didn't write this with my preferred modus operandi of "chorus first". I don't always. I make rules and then I break them! As I wish and see fit. You should too!

Another verse to write then. Where will this story go?
Since this is a tango, maybe they should meet in a dance?

Our entangled dance set the ballroom on fire
I had to make each turn in time
Or the straights would be dire
But Juan Carlos Copes has nothing on me
And here in my arms was all I could ever desire

Phew.. what? I guess the dance is a metaphor for something going on here that is serious... but to just what that is, I have no more of a clue than you. We can only guess. But that is fun to. It opens up for interpretation and misunderstanding, which includes the listener and makes them a key factor and participant in the completion of this "work of art".

I think at least our hero seem to be doing well in this somehow dire situation. I googled (remember, google is your friend), "the best Tango dancer of all times" and the name Juan Carlos Copes came up. So, I threw his name in there's a reference as for how he views his own Tango dancing capabilities.

I guess that is it. These few lines is all the lyrics we need for this one. For the middle eight I am thinking a choir thing just repeating the title, that of course will be: "Be Still My Beating Heart".

Be Still My Beating Heart

I had heard Buenos Aires was pretty in Spring
The Purple Jacaranda blossoms and the hummingbirds sing
But nothing could have prepared me
For something as beautiful as your hazel eyes

Be Still My Beating Heart
Be still and play your part
If I am to win her hand tonight
We must be in this together
Right from the start

Our entangled dance set the ballroom on fire
I had to make each turn in time
Or the straights would be dire
But Juan Carlos Copes had nothing on me
Here in my arms was I could ever desire
Be Still My Beating Heart
Be still and play your part
If I am to win her hand tonight
We must be in this together
Right from the start

Oooh...Be Still My Beating Heart
Oooh...Be Still My Beating Heart
Oooh...Be Still My Beating Heart

Be Still My Beating Heart
Be still and play your part
If I am to win her hand tonight
We must be in this together
Right from the start
We must be in this together
Right from the start

Oooh...Be Still My Beating Heart
Be Still My Beating Heart
Be still and play your part
If I am to win her hand tonight
We must be in this together
Right from the start

Oooh...Be Still My Beating Heart

Oooh...Be Still My Beating Heart
Oooh...Be Still My Beating Heart

Be Still My Beating Heart
Be still and play your part
If I am to win her hand tonight
We must be in this together
Right from the start
We must be in this together
Right from the start

Oooh...Be Still My Beating Heart

This Tango and the writing of it, is a textbook example of this Songwriting On Demand process I came up with. All I ever had to do after that was to apply it to whatever genre was at hand.

Let's sum this "method" of musical archaeology, or dissection, of any musical genre up into a series of questions:

The Mighty Questions Of This Method Of Mine:

#What bpm tempo range?
#What macro rhythm? (Straight, triplet, swing, or straight but swung)
#Are there any important accents?
#How does the groove work?
#What are the typical energy level and dynamics?
#What are typical patterns of basic instrumental elements?

What does each instrument play? What roles do they have? What is the hierarchy of importance between the instruments?
#How is the genre typically played? What is the micro timing, the dynamics... Is it sloppy or strict and tight? Slick? Angry? Laid back?
#What are the typical chords, typical harmonic content?
#What is a stylistically typical musical arrangements of parts?
#What kind of sounds?
#How is it typically produced and mixed? Slick? Rough? Dry? Wet?

Be Still My Beating Heart

Martin Carlberg

31 Cm G7 Cm C C G7
here in my arms was all I could ever desire Be still my beating heart Be
35 C C7 F Fm
still and play your part If I am to win her hand tonight
39 C G7 C C/D F/A Fm/G♯
We must be in this together Right from the start Oh Be Still My Beating Heart
43 C C/D F/A Fm/G♯ G7 C G7
Oh Be Still My Beating Heart Be Still My Beating Heart Be still
49 C C7 F Fm
and play your part If I am to win her hand tonight
53 C G7 C
We must be in this together right from the start
55 G7 C Fm G7 C
We must be in this together right from the start So Be still be still my beating heart

WHY RHYTHM IS KING

(Meaning: Why it is the most important element in music)

This may seem a bit off the writing-of-songs topic, and I would say that it both is and it isn't. It is a bit of an add-on, but I think this insight is so foundational to any and everyone who makes music in any way, shape or form, that felt impossible not to include.

AS I said in the beginning of this book, I absolutely love watching master classes. It does"t really matter what the topic is. I admit that it helps if it's a topic I am both invested and interested in, but I can often find joy in listening to a true master talk about whatever the thing might be that they have spent their entire life getting the hang of.

Something I have noticed when watching and listening to these masters, is that there are some things they have in common. I have noticed that there are some areas they focus much more on, while there are other areas that they almost collectively do not seem to take much interest to.

What I want to put forward is that they all seem to speak a great deal less about HOW to do something, and instead a whole lot more about WHY to do something. My interpretation of the meaning being that the intention behind the doing is as important or even more important than the striving for flawless execution of said deed.

Melody cannot exist without rhythm.
As soon as you sing a note after another, the two will have a rhythmic relationship that makes for one half of the melody. The first half of what makes a melody are the notes, and the second half is the rhythmic pattern of those notes.

Harmony is even less significant, since any melody can be re-harmonized indefinitely.

Another unexpected reason that proved this point, from another direction completely, was a YouTube clip of a lecture by Adam Neely called "Polyrhythms" and therein the chapter "Polyrhythms are Polypitch".

In this ground breaking lecture Neely demonstrates that when you speed up polyrhythms, you get chords.

He takes the polyrhythm of 4 against 5 against 6, just portrayed by the sound of a electronic style kick drum and speeds it up a great deal. Like magic, the sound goes from just being kick drum played in a strange pattern, to eventually turning into a blurry buzz when the high speed made it impossible to distinguish the individual hits. Then all of a sudden it happens: A perfect major chord is formed out of this bass drum pattern!

Here follows a link to that clip, well knowing that it might not be relevant when these words and these pages reach you. (The link that is.. not the clip):

https://youtu.be/-tRAkWaeepg?si=Oyo2s5AoczKnM0aS

To me this was a total revelation.
But what does it mean?
It means that all sound, at its core, is rhythm.

In this matter, I hereby rest my case.

A SONG vs A "PERFORMANCE PIECE"

This idea seems to originate from a composer/producer/musician Jon Brion. I read an interview probably back in -04 or so, where he talked about the success he was having with his original film score for the movie Eternal Sunshine Of The Spotless Mind, for which he received a Grammy.
He also spoke about this interesting way of viewing some tunes as "songs" and others as "performance pieces".

The distinction, if I understand it correctly, is made as such:

A "song" is a tune that is so fundamentally great in its basic components (lyrics, melody and chords), that it does"t really matter who is performing the song, or when it still is identifiable as a great song. It gets its point across regardless of the quality of the performance. Even if the performer is really drunk or just a bozo at a party (or a really drunk bozo at a party) everybody will nod their head, dig it and say "yep, that is an awesome song".
Come to think of it, you can in a lot of cases even exclude chords and reduce what is the actual and factual song to lyrics and melody.

A "performance piece" on the other hand, is a tune that is little or nothing on its own, but gets its power from how it is performed.
If the performance is bad, there is no musical experience to enjoy.

The example I remember he made of what is a "performance piece" was Led Zeppelin. That probably being because they were such unique performers with such highly identifiable markers: John Bonham's heavy but swinging groove... Robert Plant's screaming, wailing voice... Jimmy Page's riffing... you get the point!

Arguably, there are a lot of Led Zeppelin songs that stand on their own, without those performers, but regardless of whether Jon Brion made a good example of his own model or not, it is still interesting and has merit.

To me, examples of "songs" are classics... Dylan, Stones, The Beatles... the stuff that gets covered a lot. Songs that can be sung anywhere at any time by anybody, and still be great tunes. Like I said, it doesn't matter if the performance is at a party by drunk bozo. It will still come across as a great song. Great songs are in this way "indestructible".

"Performance pieces" on the other hand are not. For instance 12-bar blues tunes (not early stuff before it became conceptualized) have become a sort of "performance piece". To me the form of the 12-bar blues is mostly today just a vessel for expressing yourself through performance. At least it has turned into that.

A mistake is commonly and easily made here: Just because the format of a 12-bar blues is easy does not make this easy music to play well. It makes it easy music to play, but really difficult or even extremely difficult music to play well. And to make it fly? Damn. To make it really come alive, only a few can do it. Why?

Since the format is so stripped down, there is only three chords in a set 12-bar figure, and five pentatonic scale notes to use against them (there are extensions to this I know, but bear with me), you don't get much for free. If there is going to be any quality to the music it has to come from you, in this moment, right now!

So really simple, formatted songs, can be "performance pieces", because you have to fill them with content through your performance.

Funny enough, the opposite can also be true!
ANY really difficult to play (or sing) piece can be seen as a "performance piece", for obvious reasons. You have to be a fantastic performer to even carry it, or even just to get though it! With this type of piece, you get some power for free, meaning if you (and maybe your band or ensemble) get through the arrangement without fucking up, it is at least an OK rendition of the song!

> "This land is my land and this land is your land...
> .....This land was made for you and me"
>
> — *Woddy Guthire*

With a simple song arrangement, simple harmony and so on, you get nothing for free. You either express it in your own way, making it into a "Performance Piece", or the simple qualities that the song contains are so powerful that they are awesome no matter who sings and performs them. Turning them from a "Performance piece" into a "Song".

> "The answer my friend, is Blowing In The Wind
> The answer is Blowing In The Wind"
>
> — *Bob Dylan*

These lines are, to me, examples of lyrics with such fundamental qualities, that they can be sung by anyone, anywhere and anytime and still be great.
I realize that by choosing these examples I am also making an old fart of myself.

So let's take an example of the opposite direction.

When I am writing this it is the 26th of April 2023. The youngest of my three children, my almost 10 year old daughter Esther, has really gotten into this K-Pop band called "Blackpink". She listens to music a lot and right now Blackpink is on about 90 % of the time. So I have now become quite familiar with their songs, and I must say that it is quite an interesting study. I am somewhat blown away. Not by the lyrics, the melody, nor by the harmonic content, but by the production. There are hooks galore. It is really

next level stuff. The attitude in the vocal delivery is stellar and turned up to 10 in every sentence and syllable.
Are these songs quality songs without all of the fireworks? I don't think so. Maybe one or two of the tunes would survive without the tinsel and the fairy-dust, but the rest, I think not.

Which makes Blackpink an act with "Performance Piece" music more than an act with great songs.

Now, mind you, this is no value judgment. This does not lessen the worth of Blackpink tunes. It is merely a subjective observation.

Why is this interesting and how is it usable?

When I am to write a song for a specific purpose, I sometimes decide which way to go. Is this next tune going to be be a song with lyrics that are as great as I can possibly write, with a really developed melody, chords, riffs and arrangements? Or does it just need to have a nice feel in a certain way to it, and work as framework for singing a few feel good lines on and playing some tasty blues licks?
Or does I need to be a mix of both? Should it be something in between?

Mea Culpa Note: A few months have passed since I wrote the above lines about Blackpink, and I find myself not quite agreeing with myself anymore. I now think a lot of their songs are great pop songs.

But instead of re-writing or editing out those earlier lines, I kept them in and added these to show how hard it is to measure these things, and that opinions are just opinions and can change. Remember again the wise words of Dirty Harry Callahan…

> "Opinions are like assholes, everybody's got one"
>
> — *Harry Callahan*

Also, if not said clearly enough earlier, the tune "Land On My Feet", that I wrote earlier in the book is absolutely a performance piece. It is not much of a song-song, but it is instead a nice vessel for showing off your blueslicks on. And that is fun, too.

THE SENDER AND THE RECEIVER

(A little philosophical extra add on)

There is a saying, a common notion held as truth by most, that goes something like:

"Beauty is in the eye of the beholder"

And when we apply that truism to art and music, we then get:

"The beauty and power of art (and music as an expression of art), is in the eye of the beholder"

This would be, to my experience, a pretty accurate formulation of the general consensus and opinion on this matter. Although there is at least some truth to this, and although this formulation is most certainly "good enough" to hold up as an everyday mundane standpoint, it is to me, at least, not the whole truth.

It doesn't tell the whole story by far. I have this idea you see, this simple model, that I think paints a clearer picture. (Is this a "thesis", even? It is, isn't it!)

Imagine that you have two parties, the Sender and the Receiver. Let's see what they can do.

The Sender can either send a lot of information but on a narrow bandwidth.

Example: Frank Zappa

If the Receiver has his or her tuner set to this narrow band, they are in for an experience of life changing potential. But for most people, who are not tuned to this frequency, what they hear is just a sort of.......................... noise.

Or...

The Sender can also send a lot of information on a wide bandwidth.

Example: The Beatles, Queen

Sending on a wide band will means a greater number of people will be receptive. Music that sends a lot of information widely, will be a sure hit and have often have great lasting power. Therefor, just HOW you send a lot of info on a wide band is a riddle yet to be solved.
A very small group of artists, writers and producers have been able to tap into this source, this muse, but brie y and only intuitively.
No one has yet figured out the exact formula for this.

Thirdly,

The Sender can send little information, but on a wide bandwidth.

This is where we find some superficial pop stuff. That music that sounds nice and doesn't disturb anyone. This is the music will never strike anyone like a bolt of lightning. The music where no ones life will be pushed into a whole new trajectory just upon hearing it.
But it is is all good. The whole spectrum of music is needed, from as deep as the Mariana Trench to as shallow as a puddle. It is the same thing with every form of artistic expression.
Painted art has everything from wallpaper patterns to Leonardo Da Vinci. Written art spans the range from Comic Books to Fjodor Dostoevsky. This is the music that is here today but replaced by music sounding just the same but different tomorrow.

Fourthly and lastly,
The Sender can send little information on a narrow bandwidth.
This is simply failed music. All failed art falls under this category. The Sender fails to transmit, and there is nothing for anyone to receive but noise and static.

There it is. My thesis of "The Sender and The Reciever" .

What it means is, that even though perhaps the eye of the beholder does not see beauty, that doesn't mean that beauty is not being sent. All it says is that the owner of the eye, the Receiver, does not have his or her tuner, frequency and bandwidth, set up in such a manner, to be able to receive what is being transmitted. So, if somebody doesn't like your music, it need not say anything about its inherent qualities, only that they are not being received.

Same thing if you don't like something. It might just be you who is failing to receive.

HOW TO READ A BRIEF

This chapter could just as well have been called "How to DECIPHER a Brief", judging on how remarkably difficult my students often find this task.

When being asked to write something, and you receive a brief containing the information on the music that is being commissioned, the first question to be asked, in my mind, is:

"Who is the client?"

For instance:

Is it a publishing company seeking material for a specific artist or a type of artist? Is it for TV or film? Is it a company wanting music for a commercial?

Let us divide this into client categories...

"**The Publishing company**" or "**The Artist**"

Sometimes you might be asked to write something directly for an artist. One great benefit of working directly with the artist, him-or herself, is that it eliminates the guess work, and you will be getting feedback directly from the source.

Otherwise the publisher has to guess what the artist wants, and then you have to guess what the publisher wants by guessing what they are guessing that the artist wants. Phew!

There is a lot of room for mistakes in there, would you not agree?
My methodology though, remains the same:

#What style of music is asked for?
#What are the elements of that style?
#What are the building blocks?
#What type of language is used? Is it hard ghetto slang or formal, posh-sounding English or what?
#What topics does lyrics in this style typically address?
#What production style is most common?
#What instruments and sounds are commonly employed?
#What type of sound aesthetics?

From publishers you will often get reference music.

They might say: "Write in the style of these songs".

From a publisher you also might get references that are tracks from other artists than the artist your song or songs is intended for, if the publisher wants to push or at least nudge the artist in a certain creative direction.

Some artists will also do this, send you tracks to write in

style of, that is, while many are instead quite sensitive to the idea of admitting that they look to other artists for inspiration and direction.

Another question: should you only look to the clichés? Should you only look to what that style of music is doing right NOW? Where it is at in it's evolution NOW? Or should you think of where it might go NEXT? That depends on how bold you are. Only looking to the history of the style and even where it is currently at, is of course, the safer play.

Trying to expand on the style, thinking one step ahead of the times you live in, is obviously a risky thing, and can easily blow up in your face. But then again, it can absolutely also be worth it. In that case you will really impressed every one by showing that you the chosen one who is one step ahead of the game.

It is up to you.
Sometimes, if you are on a roll, try to write more than one. Write one safe and one daring, but maybe not present them at the same time but instead one at the time. First the safe to see how it lands, then the bold and daring one.
Good titles are also really important and not to be underestimated. Good titles give a strong first impression and they are indeed important.

Also, although both publishers and artists work with songs on a daily basis, this does NOT necessarily mean that they have a producer's ear. Most don't. It is crazy but true. What I mean by them not having a "producer's ear" is:

Don't play them shitty demos and expect them to see the potential of the song. They most probably won't.

To me, a producer's ear is the skill to hear many possible and results even from a rough demo.

Most people, even veterans in the music business, don't have this skill, and therefor they must be presented with a demo that is as finished a product as possible.
The demo needs to represent the important selling points of the song as well as possible.

Sometimes it is a song that is only supposed to be played with a simple guitar or piano, and then of course that is how it needs to be presented, but if it is supposed to be a more elaborately instrumented and produced song, all the important elements need to be there when you present the demo.

If possible, you should even present the actual intended finished production of the song, where the artist can simply swap the demo vocals for his or her own and then send it to mix and master.

If the publisher has told you which artist the song is for, or if you are working directly with the artist, try reading up on the artist. Learn as much as you can about them in order to write songs with titles and topics they will easily relate to. Listen in on their vocal range and try to get the key right. I once read an artist's autobiography to find stuff, and waddaya know, she loved both the songs I sent her! She felt that I had somehow read her mind" and shown that in the lyrics.

Let's write a song on a made up brief of this kind. I will choose a genre that I am not completely at home with. Modern R'n'B.

I realize that since this is a made up situation, and even If I try to find contemporary tunes to work as references, they too will be dated when this book comes out (or today since I don't keep up with what is hip), and even more so with each passing day after that.

So, judge the song by the comparison of the reference tracks I will come up with, and if you think from that perspective the track might have been right for this made up artist.

It is totally hypothetical, I understand. It's just an exercise.

(I'm telling this to myself in order to relieve some pressure.)

Today is November 24th, 2023, and I choose three random, current R'n'B songs from a Spotify top list. They are:

We Might Even Be Falling In Love – Victoria Monét, Bryson Tiller
Change – FLO
Softest Touch – Khalid

Ok, let us say these songs are references in my brief. We

will play the game that I am commissioned to write a song in the style of these the songs.

The song cannot be a rip off. It must hold its own.

Listening through them I am pleasantly surprised though. They are quite classic at first glance. A lot of ornamented chords and sophisticated changes over a danceable groove. So let's do this.

Browsing through my little leather book of lyrical ideas my eyes are drawn to this simple phrase for a title: "Can I Come Over Tonight"

First, I'll just give the lyrics in the chorus a go.

I am hearing it like this:

Can I Come Over Tonight
Please say "Yes you can"
Can I Come Over right now
Please say "Yes you can"
Can I Come Over
And make sweet love to you
Can I Come Over that's all that I wanna do

It's not the deepest Leonard Cohen poetry. But R'n'B most often isn't about that. The genre is mainly about feel. Ultimately I dear even say, it is a whole genre about sex.

In other words, these lines work..

So, what is this story? Who wants to come over to whom, and where are we? This line comes to me:

Who decided the bars around here should close this early

Ok. So, somebody is out on a drinking spree. Why? Heartache? Maybe. But since I am in a positive mood, why not instead imagine that this someone has met someone he or she has taken a fancy to, but hasn't yet, for some reason, had the guts to act upon it. Let us continue....

Who decided the bars around here should close this early
I haven't had nearly enough to drink your smile away

I am setting myself up for trouble having to match and rhyme these long lines...

Who decided the bars around here should close this early
I haven't had nearly enough to drink your smile away
I know you're not supposed to call this late
But still I am
Laying my heart on the line

That's a first verse right there. I feel ready to go into the chorus, so we don't need a pre-chorus

Can I Come Over Tonight
Please say "Yes you can"
Can I Come Over right now
Please say "!Yes you can"
Can I Come Over
And make sweet love on you
Can I Come Over that's what I wanna do

Let's keep it simple for now. The phrase "love on you" I heard Ray Charles sing at sometime, and after googling it, it shows up as a perfectly legit slang term that means something like "to shower somebody with love". Maybe I will have the guts to use "Love on you" instead of "Love to you". We'll see.

(I realize that using Ray Charles style slang might probably be a case of "Cultural Appropriation", but if we are truthful, isn't that really the case as soon as we write in any genre not based in our own culture)

What is the moral of the story, and where is it going? Does our hero get a "yes"? A green light to mosey on over? I think so. Absofreakinglutely. Feels way better and makes for more of a feelgood story than him or her getting a "NO", yes?

Then how to continue in the ever dreaded second verse? Where should we be at in this storyline?

Oh but wait... how about this idea... Why not make this a duet?

Why not in the second verse into the other persons view. And that other person is at home, having the same kind of thoughts of our hero… and just when he or she is about to call, our hero calls that very moment! Simple, nothing super special, but fun.

I think it is interesting to consider which part should be sung by whom, male or female? Pardon me for being a bit gender normative. I am a heterosexual male finding myself writing from a heterosexual normative perspective, I realize this. But I am writing from what I know and do not have anything but the greatest respect for people who do not represented within that norm. So please bear with me with the gender norm thing. And also keep in mind that even though I write from this perspective, the listener do not know that and can interpret and envision these characters any way he or she wants to.

The first thought was that the first verse is the male and then the second verse is the female. It seems classic to paint the picture that he is out bar hopping and she is at home being a good girl, but for obvious reasons that feels a bit stale and cliché. There is a feeling of "nothingness" to it. And isn't it is a crappy thing that just by doing a switch of roles here, boom.. the lyric idea feels more potent. Maybe, hopefully... this is a generational question and simply a matter that you might not recognize if you are a great deal younger than me (I was born in the early seventies), and maybe this issue is no longer present in your world.

So we will flip the script and go with the idea that she's out drinking and thinking about him. He's at home thinking about her. She wants to come over. She's the one doing the booty call. Also, I think the type of language and topic feels genre appropriate for R'n'B, yes?

Note: I had to scrap this nice duet idea for practical and time-in-studio reasons, but the idea is still valid. Maybe that version will see the light of day later down the line.

So now we instead put the more easy to pull off version of the story and the song on like it was a well worn t-shirt, and the second verse now goes on like this:

An un-reliable source said:
"Cool guys wait at least a week before they call back"
Not to be needy and not to give himself away
So I know I'm not supposed to call you
Yet here I am
Holding my heart in my hands

Can I Come Over
Please say "Yes you can"
Can I Come Over tonight
Please say "Yes you can"
Can I Come Over
And make sweet love to you
that's what I wanna do

After that I feel like having a solo over a slightly different chord vamp and then into the final chorus.

Can I Come Over
"Yes you can"
Can I Come Over tonight
"Yes you can"
Can I Come Over
And show my love for you. Please tell me

"You can come over"
Oh say it again
"You can come over tonight"
Let me hear it again
"You can come over"
And make sweet love to you
"That's what I want you to do"
Then that's what we're gonna do

The arrangement of the parts in the song then goes like this:

I (Intro)

A

B
A
B
C (solo)
B
B

Can I Come Over

Who decided the bars around here should close this early
I haven't had enough to drink your smile away
I know you're not supposed to call this late
But still I am, laying my heart on the line

Can I Come Over
Please say "Yes you can"
Can I Come Over tonight
Please say "Yes you can"
Can I Come Over
And make sweet love to you
That's what I wanna do

An un-reliable source said:
"Cool guys wait at least a week before they call back"
Not to be needy and not to give themselves away
So I know I'm not supposed to call you
Yet here I am, holding my heart in my hands

Can I Come Over
Please say "Yes you can"
Can I Come Over Tonight
Please say "Yes you can"
Can I Come Over
And make sweet love on you
That's what I wanna do

Solo

Can I Come Over
"Yes you can"
Can I Come Over tonight
"Yes you can"
Can I Come Over
And show my love for you
Please tell me

"You can come over"
Oh say it again
"You can come over tonight"
Let me hear it again
"You can come over"
And make sweet love to you
"That's what I want you to do"
Then that's what we're gonna do

Can I Come Over

Martin Carlberg

40 B^7 Em^7 A$^{7(sus4)}$ A^7

I know I´m not supposed to call you Yet here I am

43 Am^7 D^{11} D C^{maj7}

Holding my heart in my hands Can I Come Over Please say yes

46 G^{maj7} C^{maj7} G^{maj7}

I can Can I come over tonight Please say yes I can Can I come

49 C^{maj7} Em^7 F^{maj7} E^7/G# E^7 Am D$^{7(sus4)}$ D^7

over And make sweet love on you That´s all that I wanna do

53 C^{maj7} Em^7 D C^{maj7} Em^7 G/D D C^{maj7} Em^7 D C^{maj7} Em^7 Em^7/D D Em^7/D

61 D C^{maj7} G^{maj7}

Can I Come Over Yes you can Can I

64 C^{maj7} G^{maj7} C^{maj7}

come over tonight Yes you can Can I come over And

67 Em^7 F^{maj7} E^7/G# E^7 Am D$^{7(sus4)}$ D^7 C^{maj7}

show my love for you You can come over

71 G^{maj7} C^{maj7} G^{maj7} C^{maj7}

You can come over now You can come over And

75 Em^7 F^{maj7} E^7/G# E^7 Am^7 F#m Am^7

make sweet love to you That´s what I want you to do

79 D$^{7(sus4)}$ D G^{maj7} G^{maj7}

Then that´s what we´re gonna do

WRITING FOR TV OR FILM

This is of course another subject far too big to even come close to covering properly here.
It needs a book or a series of books on it's own.

So how to sum this up in a short chapter in a way that still has some relevance? Impossible.

Also, is it a classical score? Any other type of other instrumental music, or is there to be vocals? Or all of the above? All I can or will do, is just to open the lid on this box that is film music, write a few lines and leave it at that.

Let us say that we have been asked to write for a film.

A nice way of looking at it, compelling at least to me, is the idea of writing the music not just as a commentary to what you see on the screen, but rather to adress and write to the subtext of the story. Therefor we ask the crucial question: "What is the film really about?". What is the abstraction of the story or the boiled down deeper meaning? For example, Christopher Nolan one day, out of the blue, asked Hans Zimmer to write a musical theme about a father's love for his daughter. No more info was given than that.
So Zimmer did just that. A good while later, Nolan revealed that it was for his new movie project, "Interstellar".

So that is what I am talking about.

All the space grandeur aside, "Interstellar" is about a father's love for his daughter, and the main theme was written about that idea. Then, to make the theme work in the context of an epic space-film, the theme was played on the largest instrument known to man, which also produces the largest sound known to man, namely the church organ. Another Hans Zimmer example is his Batman theme. He wrote a new theme when Christopher Nolan (the very same) took over the franchise. Zimmer thought that the previous theme, written by Danny Elfman, was too "melodically developed" to represent Bruce Wayne, a person "stuck" or "frozen" in a moment he can't get out of. That moment is of course the trauma of witnessing his parents being shot in the street by a robber after they had to leave an opera on account of young Bruce behaving badly. So the trauma and the guilt of being the reason they were in that alley at exactly that time, fixes him like super-glue to that moment and the emotions attached to it.

Therefore according to Hans Zimmer, he cannot have this melodically fully developed hero-theme. Zimmer's Batman theme, on these artistic grounds, consists of only two notes. Like something is stuck. Awesome.

Danny Elfman (also a great composer, make no mistake) wrote for what we see, the heroic and larger than life Batman, resulting in an epic, fully developed hero- theme. Hans Zimmer wrote to the subtext. A person acting super-hero heroic, but is at the same time having an underdeveloped, "stuck" psyche, resulting in a grandiose sounding theme but with only two notes to represent this.

YET another Hans Zimmer story is his Sherlock Holmes Theme.

He based it on his idea of how he thought a mind like Holmes would work. That doesn't make leaps of assumption, and therefore the melody cannot make any leaps. That the master detective's mind systematically and step-by-step makes its way forward, ever closing in on an inevitable conclusion. So Zimmer's Sherlock Holmes Theme is a really neat and clever chromatic melody. I love it.
Again:

Writing for film is a massive undertaking and needs its own 600-page book. Or a bunch of 600-page books.

(Are you noticing my reluctance to even *try* to address this immense topic?)

Back to the attempt:

So, we write to the subtext. Or not. If the sum of the parts is supposed to be simple and upfront, then we will deliver just that and write music that supports what is there, in plain sight on the screen. Take for example the old silent movies that had a live pianist accompanying the happenings on the screen. Or any mix of the two vantage points, as per what is asked for or needed.

How to know which way to go? For starters, from the very first meeting, listen very closely to everything the director says. The values and strong descriptive words he or she is clear about are important, but also for subtle information and clues and cues he or she is giving away without knowing it. Take notes. Write stuff down.

Sometimes there is "Temp Music". This is of course short for "Temporary Music" Temp Music is both a blessing and a curse.
A blessing, because you get a perfectly clear picture of what the director likes and is looking for. A curse, because the bar might be set high in composition,
performance and production. Often they can also be quite attached to it giving you a tall order to top, let's say "The Imperial March" by John Williams.

A trend (as per today 2023) in movie scoring, is to stay well and clear away from melody. I think it is an unfortunate trend that makes for bland and forgettable music. I believe the reason for it might be that since melodies carry so much information, they will either be spot-on in conveying, enhancing and evoking the appropriate emotions for what is seen on the screen, or it will be completely off. Since the odds are against being spot-on, movie makers play it safe and shy away from melody, opting for more abstract music that can be applied less riskily.

WRITING FOR A MUSIC LIBRARY

(Royalty free or not)

Brace yourself for some shameless bragging:
I got this "Key Player" award from the royalty free music library Epidemic Sound:

I partially got it (I think), for my 99,73% "approval rate", meaning that of all the material I submitted, they approved and bought 99,73%. And the only tunes they didn't take were rejected right in the beginning, when I was just getting the hang of it. After that my score was 100%.
You would have to say, regarding how to relate to a music library, or at least this particular music library, I seemed to have cracked the code. But times and things change, and the way I approached this type of work only a few years ago, might in some cases be way off today. Still in some ways people are always people, the basics and fundamentals of that doesn't really change, so I think there still might be some take aways here. For starters, music libraries use and sell music in so many different ways today.

When I started writing for them, the main part of their business came from TV use. Some shows today can use 30 to 40 different little snippets of different songs and pieces of music to enhance the mood of a scene, and to license all of them was an ever growing hassle. Add to that, the hassle of different countries licensing the show, multiple seasons, re-runs and so on.

So, the basic business idea from the music libraries was to simplify this licensing process by eliminating it. Then, as the libraries' catalogue grew, new ideas of possible markets naturally followed. Next new market to arise was what was called first "In Store Radio" and later "In Store Music", where the library offers an alternative for malls, stores, gas stations, hair salons and so on for having background music playing in their establishments at a lower cost than when using ”regular radio music”. Further development came when companies started getting the music to their commercials from libraries instead of having original music written for them.

YouTubers finding music here at low cost have become a big, big thing since there are 982475479209205757 of them out there. And so it goes… Forever finding more ways to create value with the acquired music catalogue, by the day. The way I approached writing for music libraries was this:

First of all, in these cases, I have zero ego. My personal preferences can and should mean nothing. A viewpoint can be argued that bringing your own subjective taste out of the equation is impossible, and this is, of course, absolutely true, but doing so was at least my intention. I try to be as “subjectively objective” as possible. As in, “what decision will make the music meet the brief in as good a way as possible” over ”what is the most interesting musical choice to ME right now”.
Or, as comic genius Groucho Marx said:

"Those are my principles, and if you don’t like them... well I have others"

Secondly, when working with Music Libraries, clichés are your friend. In 99 cases out of 100, the music is meant to work behind moving picture, amplifying, supporting and clarifying emotional content in said moving pictures. Therefore, the music has to have a clear intent. The

emotions they are meant to convey need to be crystal clear and direct. The person in charge of choosing the right music for the TV-show they are producing can search for music with a certain mood, and find your music, and when put in place with the picture content, it will work as intended. Of course, there is a place and a use for the abstract, indefinable piece of music as well, but it will be roughly 200 times harder to sell such a piece to a music library, than a piece that is in the middle of the genre that is commissioned in the brief and delivers an immediate emotional response.
So don't try to re-invent the wheel here.

Use this work to learn about musical genres. What makes them tick? What makes them work.? Add to your musical bag of tricks. Add to your repertoire.
Learn how different genres need to be played, mixed, arranged and produced.

Learn also to take criticism. It can be direct and brutal.

Grow a skin thicker than a rhino's.

You should even make a conscious effort to expect the client to be blunt and forthright about what they want, and if and how and in what way, the music you are presenting does not match that expectation. It is within their rights and they do not need to always sugarcoat that message in order not to bruise a tender ego. So get used to it. Expect it even.

Also. Do you see how that just came full circle?

If you keep your ego out of it, your ego can't be bruised by harsh criticism.

For all of you reading this as an E-Book, here are some links to Music Library music that I have done

https://open.spotify.com/track/0icSujRETlmJRt8i4gfLQi?si=39dfd910585e4195

https://open.spotify.com/track/5NybDff2KT68lRuvwfGPYd?si=79e9e653360 44922

https://open.spotify.com/track/4nXVSbMzlVn08z3bsb7?si=2bdaeb763f7b477b

https://open.spotify.com/track/6RsyyTgPmeBk2kZj7lPJ6U?si=e3989cfb39f545f7

https://open.spotify.com/track/4lrHPyUmZouL5NYI8kGMU1?si=6a088cb032 364f0b

https://open.spotify.com/track/2rSXk0liGQatech8g4Sov0?si=b258d13b82294b9f

https://open.spotify.com/track/05P3Go9jycx7kNt6z6o62x?si=3838e9767d26413 3

https://open.spotify.com/track/6y0KPUWpijed8CQX0fYArT?si=0cdbfed485af 43ab

https://open.spotify.com/track/2ZIYGYwMPeZ2otWqXI9but?si=b0f502a1bb 6049bf

https://open.spotify.com/track/2rSXk0liGQatech8g4Sov0?si=b258d13b82294b9f

WRITING FOR A COMMERCIAL

When approached by a company to write a song or an instrumental piece for a commercial, I think there are a few obvious first questions to ask in the first conversation with the client:

#What are the main values that the company wants to convey?
#What feelings do they want the music to convey?
#What is the factual service or product to be marketed?

Ask for the key words of the above points. But on top of that, listen extremely carefully and be sure to take notes while they talk. Often, there is more nuance to be found in the way that they talk about the product or campaign, than in the words they use. They often tell you more than they think they are telling you.
Everybody "leaks" information. Also:

#Is there reference music? Same as "Temp Music", but for some reason the lingo often differs)

Reference or temp music is, again, both a blessing and a curse.
A blessing, because it gives you a perfectly defined starting

point in something that you know for sure they like. A curse, because it often narrows your manoeuvring space. The music you come up with might have to resemble their reference or they won't like it.

THE FORCE OR STANDING IN YOUR OWN SHOES

(Another little philosophical extra add on)

> "Songwriting is an art unto itself, not to be confused with performing."
>
> —*Joe Stafford*

The connection between this following part and what it means to be a songwriter is... somewhat far fetched, but in my mind, still there. I first wasn't going to include this part, but now I guess I am, nonetheless. So I am not going to explain this, but instead leave it up to you to connect the dots between the following thoughts and songwriting.

You see, I have this theory about what it takes to be a great performer.

Not just a good performer mind you, that is something else, but a GREAT performer. Let us say these following are the key ingredients of being a performer:

Talent

Talent is a very abstract and imprecise word. What is talent? Is it always this one singular thing, or can what it is differ from person to person? I think it absolutely can, and does. It might mean that you have access to a ow of creative ideas.

It can also mean an aptitude for understanding how these ideas can be brought into this world and manifested through the use of your voice or your body or through the use of musical instruments.

Skills

Skills are both acquired and to some extent given for free through talent.

Somebody extremely talented, can with sometimes minimal practice coax beautiful music out of an instrument they saw for the first time just moments ago.

Somebody with less or even minimal talent, can practice this (or any) musical instrument for years or even a lifetime without ever really making music with the sounds coming from the efforts. They can learn to PLAY, but what comes out just isn't music, but... noise. When on the other hand, somebody with a good deal of talent, is also willing to put in the time, and practice, then great things can happen. And one could easily believe and think that that outcome is then a given. But alas, no.

There are many ways to drive that car off the road. With both talent, and the willingness to put in the time and effort to practice and learn the craft, the result is always that that person becomes good or even really good at what they do. Often good enough to make a profession out of it.

So why are so few GREAT then? Wherein lies the key to greatness? I can at least present you with an idea. True or false, you be the judge.

I think the keys are courage and intention.

Every day we all put our clothes on, and with them, we also put on the game face of life. The version of yourself that others get to meet. This is nothing bad in and of itself, it is a practical necessity. It is a social tool we use in personal and professional relationships. One way to see it is that we put our skills and social skills "in front of ourselves". I think we must have all met people with simply perfect social skills, who still leave us with no clue to who they really ARE. A feeling of, "behind all of that, who is the real YOU?"

The same thing, that same effect, is what happens when somebody doesn't make the quantum leap (or the leap of faith), from good to great. GOOD: Is when you use your skills as a presentation version of yourself. You put your skills in front of yourself. All the while you hide behind your internal walls.

People will meet your skills, your game face. They will meet your presentable version of yourself, not the real you, not the essence of you. Why? Because it is scary to reveal yourself. It is much safer this way. It is easier also this way to be more consistently good. Since you don't get that creative, you stay well within your comfort zone and always deliver what is expected of you.

We have all heard these performers.

The singer with the fantastic voice, but nothing really stirs inside when he or she sings. Or the player of any musical instrument that plays all the nice butter notes, but never makes you want to neither dance nor cry.

GREATNESS: Is a thing far more interesting than being GOOD . The first version of greatness is easy to grasp and understand. It is when all pieces of the puzzle are present. The performer is:

#Greatly talented
Has devoted their life to study of music as a whole and their instrument of choice. These studies need not be in a school or any kind of institution, but they are studies, nevertheless.

Here comes the water diviner, the most important piece of the puzzle:

#Has the courage not to filter the creative signal in order to cater to or simply please an audience. He or she plays what is in their heart and soul.
Thus, we get to meet this performer's true self. They have the guts to stand in their shoes. They play or sing from their heart and are unafraid of the audience's judgment. Or at least, not so afraid that they would ever refrain from being this honest.

This, like I said, was the first kind of greatness. The easy one to understand. The second one is the interesting one.

It seems to me, that this courage, to dare to be this naked and honest in front of other people, is a very rare trait indeed.

At the same time, it is so powerful, that it goes a long way by itself. Well, at least *almost* by itself.

All by itself, i.e. without talent or skills, you get that person we have all cringed at... who is utterly convinced they are great, and performs their heart out, but we can all see, that they have nothing. Nothing.

BUT. Combine that courage with raw talent, and even minus highly developed skills, you can still have GREATNESS!! Isn't this the most interesting, amazing thing?

We all know and love them (well, not everybody does). The singer that can't sing really straight or on pitch, but has an honesty that melts hearts. The songwriter that writes beautiful lyrics, and though narrating more than singing delivers them as being the truth of all truths. The front man or woman who can't really dance by any standardized norm, but dances their heart out just the same, winning everybody over. Can Mick Jagger really dance? Does he have a traditionally pretty voice?

In a traditional sense, perhaps not, but for me, he is one of the best singers and performers to ever get up on a stage, as well as being one of the best writers. One of the best everything.

Could Tina Turner really dance? No matter what your answer to that question is, I think that she was irresistible. The most awesome of the awesomest.

So, to me, can they sing and dance? Yes. Hell yes. Expression over skill. Expression over skill. Expression over skill. Every. Time. And to be expressive is in a way its own skill.

This also resolves the fight between virtuosity and feeling. The argument that virtuosos don't play with feeling, and that simple and sloppy players somehow do.
Can the truth of the matter be that simple players, who are very limited in their skills, don't have the option or possibility to place these limited skills "in front of themselves", and thereby have no other alternative but to invest all their

feelings into their playing in order for SOMETHING to come out, will more often than not sound heartfelt and honest?

Virtuosos on the other hand, have the option to hide behind their skills, and many do.

There are also, of course, fantastic virtuosos who play with both tons of feeling and impeccable chops.

While on the subject of virtuosity, let me say:

Isn't it all misunderstood?

The way we usually and normally refer to a virtuoso, we often seem to refer to their technical prowess but is not the point of playing music on an instrument to convey and make people feel something? Anything, really? So should the virtuoso, then, do just that?

Shouldn't they perform with skill and precision, no matter whether he or she chooses to play technically intricate music with a lot of notes, or more simply structured music with only a few notes?
Should not the person that can convey or "send" a lot of information with only a few notes, be viewed as the greater virtuoso?

If you think about it, how many players are there that can play really technically advanced pieces, and be great at it? Quite a few. But how many are truly great at making the music come alive with just a few simple notes masterfully timed, with just the right dynamics, with just the right everything, completely intuitively, in the moment? Just a handful. Fewer than few.

I hereby claim, for the record, that I consider it as hard, or even harder to convey a lot of emotional information through simplicity than through complexity.
If you compare it to spoken or written word, do we ever remember the one that talks the most? Uses the most words? No.

So in the case of spoken or written word we have gotten further in the development of an understanding here.

In this case, we rightfully celebrate the people who can, in a simple short phrase, capture something profound.

We pay more attention to the people who can see and capture the reflection of the universe in a glass of water, than to the ones that ramble on and on trying to make the glass of water the universe.
So, in my mind, B.B. King was a virtuoso. If you use the definition my way.

Although his playing often meant playing one note for a full solo (almost), he managed to convey more emotional information with that single note, than 99,999999999% of all other guitarist do with their with all their combined notes and in their whole lifetime.

That is virtuosity.

Let's get back to the idea of intent, just a few notes more.. The intent to perform, or to make any kind of art really, can greatly differ. Often, this is also a matter of maturity. The young person wants to impress. "Look what I can do!" This has to do with simple, natural feelings of insecurity.
It is not entirely without musical merit, but serves more as a display of the ego of the performer, looking to win the audience over by impressing them.

The drawback of that "strategy" is that being impressed is a very brief "high". First there is an small explosion of feelings... a "WOW!!!", but if there is no substance to what is being sent, no "sustain" to the signal, that wow feeling passes very quickly. After that, usually, comes the feeling of "NEXT!"

Then the young person wanting to impress, matures (hopefully). They grow up and realize they don't really have to impress anybody. They slowly start looking for a deeper well within themselves to draw from.

To me, that deeper well tells me to write songs, record songs and perform those songs in front of a crowd, just because. Just because of what? I don't know. You tell me. Just because it feels good, perhaps. And just because you feel good doing it, others might feel good, too.

What "feeling good" actually means is also relative. Not every feeling of worth is "happy-go-lucky".

That is not exactly what I mean by "feeling good" here. I

mean to say that every feeling of release is essentially good. Do we not want the full range of emotions? Is the good as good without the occasional bad?

To me, the greatness lies in drawing from a deep well of artistic need for expression, and performing without second guessing what the audience might want or like. This will mean that what comes out is actually something others might enjoy.

I think that concludes my small endeavour of writing a book on this musical topic. There is so much more to say. Endlessly so, but for now, this is where I will stop. Thank you for the time you have spent with my words, and I sincerely hope you took something away from the effort...

Best Wishes
Martin Carlberg

Addendum:

When I started writing this book maybe two and a half years ago, this matter that I will now briefly address was not in this regard yet an issue. But since then things are moving and developing at nearly the speed of light in this field. And now it is starting to be a thing impossible to leave unaddressed. That is also why I point out that I am inserting this text as an addendum, instead of just writing it in. I am of course talking about AI.

When I am writing this it is May 7th 2024. Yesterday I gave the two allegedly best AI sites for writing songs a try. And exactly in the same way that you can just type in a prompt and get a picture, we are all already used to that, and lately do the same and get a lifelike video (insane!!), you can now from a prompt get a song. Completely produced and ready for release. At first glimpse, this is the beginning of the end. The first listen to some of these songs I rendered, gave me a sense of...WTF???!!!!

But already by the second listen, it started to fall apart. And by the third listen I had "seen through it", and no longed felt anything for it. And it is not the sound or anything like that. It is, in my mind, the lack of... Intention. And thereby the lack of, in a perhaps more cliché word, soul. Will this change the industry? Yes. I think so. Will it render the role of the songwriter moot? I think, on the contrary, it will not.

It will for sure change things up though.
If I am to make any kind of prediction, I will guess that the more generic, mainstream and "shallow" the music is, or any other form of art for that matter, AI will probably be able to replace such "wear and tear" art very soon. But as soon as you or me or anyone, create from will, lust and intent, we are already in that instance doing something AI cannot. Not until it becomes GAI, anyway. That means General Artificial Intelligence. Which basically means that it has become an conscious entity. At which case we might be fucked either way. But, as long as it is not, we can do things with our intention that AI absolutely cannot. So the most generic music can suffer a setback. Also the

most generic production might meet this fate. What then, does that say about a book like "Songwriting On Demand", and all the techniques I put forward in these pages?

I think that when the dust settles, things might in a way be for the better. That what we human beings can do will be held in higher regard than before. But it might get worse before it gets better. As always, we must test something new out and take it to it's limits before we know what it can and can not do, and be rational about it.

It is the same phenomena as everywhere else in our society, a lot of situations where people meet people are being replaced with digital solutions that are more both time and cost efficient. But I think that the pendulum will swing back the other way. Many companies are going to want to profile themselves not long in the future as people-meeting-people friendly.
And art is no different. In the end, to receive an experience that will have intent and meaning and make a lasting impression. There must be a "meeting" of sorts between the artist and the "fan". Between the sender and the receiver.

The future will definitely be interesting to say the least, but I remain positive and hopeful. And I think ultimately, that you and me both, should only concern ourselves with being the best sender of the best content with the and best intentions. Then these laws of Sender and Receiver will sort out the rest.
/Martin